LETTERS TO YOU

LETTERS TO YOU

Words of support and inspiration
for difficult times

JAZZ
THORNTON

PENGUIN BOOKS

PENGUIN

UK | USA | CANADA | IRELAND | AUSTRALIA
INDIA | NEW ZEALAND | SOUTH AFRICA | CHINA

PENGUIN IS AN IMPRINT OF THE PENGUIN RANDOM HOUSE GROUP OF COMPANIES,
WHOSE ADDRESSES CAN BE FOUND AT GLOBAL.PENGUINRANDOMHOUSE.COM.

Penguin
Random House
New Zealand

FIRST PUBLISHED BY PENGUIN RANDOM HOUSE NEW ZEALAND, 2022

1 3 5 7 9 10 8 6 4 2

TEXT © JAZZ THORNTON, 2022, UNLESS OTHERWISE CREDITED

DESIGN BY CAT TAYLOR © PENGUIN RANDOM HOUSE NEW ZEALAND
AUTHOR PHOTOGRAPH BY MADDIE GRAEME
PREPRESS BY IMAGE CENTRE GROUP
PRINTED AND BOUND IN CHINA BY TOPPAN LEEFUNG PRINTING LIMITED

A CATALOGUE RECORD FOR THIS BOOK IS AVAILABLE FROM THE NATIONAL LIBRARY OF NEW ZEALAND.

ISBN 978-0-14-377661-1
EISBN 978-0-14-377662-8
ISBN (AUDIO) 978-0-14-377767-0

PENGUIN.CO.NZ

MIX
Paper from
responsible sources
FSC® C104723

Contents

Introduction 8

Part 1: Emotions 13

To read when you are feeling angry 14

To read when you are feeling anxious 19

    Anxiety — tips and tools 24

To read when you are feeling guilty 27

    Guilt — tips and tools 31

To read when you are experiencing depression 32

To read when you are feeling sad 36

    Sadness — tips and tools 40

To read when you are having a good day 42

To read when you are struggling with grief 46

Part 2: Experiences 51

To read when you are feeling alone 52

    Feeling alone — tips and tools 57

To read when you are feeling stressed 58

To read when you are feeling overwhelmed 64

    Feeling overwhelmed — tips and tools 70

To read when you are having suicidal thoughts 72

    50 reasons to stay 79

To read when you are feeling actively suicidal 82

    Feeling actively suicidal — tips and tools 88

To read when you are feeling impulsive 94

To read when you are having trouble with food 100

To read when you have the urge to self-harm 104

    Self-harm — tips and tools 107

To read when you have relapsed 108

To read when you are struggling with trauma 112

    Struggling with trauma and flashbacks — tips and tools 118

To read when you feel like you are slipping into old habits 120

To read when you are struggling to sleep 124

Part 3: Beliefs 131

To read when you feel like a burden 132

To read when you don't feel like you are enough 139

To read when you are feeling unlovable 145

To read when you feel like there is no hope 150

Part 4: Help 161

To read if you are a parent 162

To read if you have a friend who is struggling 170

To read if you are scared to tell your parents how you are feeling 175

To read if you are scared to see a professional 180

To read if you are afraid to see your doctor for help 184

To read if you feel like your struggles aren't as bad as other people's 191

One final letter 195

Where to get help 198

Toolbox of handy skills to use when in distress 201

Acknowledgements 220

Introduction

Dear you,

Welcome. I am so glad that you have picked up this book —
whether you bought it for yourself or someone else has bought
it for you, I am so glad that you have it in your hands. This
book is a little different from anything I have done before,
but it is something that I am hoping will provide you with
comfort and hope, and enable you to feel a little less alone in
the journey.

Life is such a rollercoaster. It can throw us all kinds of
things, from positive experiences to trauma, from good times
to difficulties. Through this book, I want to ensure that no
matter what you are feeling or experiencing, you know that
you are not in this thing by yourself.

For those of you who don't know me, my name is Jazz
Thornton. I am a mental health activist from New Zealand,
and I try to live every day to help others. I have had my own
fair share of struggles in life, from early childhood sexual
abuse, to severe mental illness, which had me in and out
of hospitals and psych wards. I have been homeless, made
many mistakes, destroyed relationships (and restored them).

I battled with many debilitating beliefs about myself, and spent a lot of my life thinking that I was the only one who felt like this and that the world would be better without me in it. You can read about my own journey in my first book, 'Stop Surviving, Start Fighting', if you want to know more.

This book was inspired by a friend of mine named Cahlia. Back in 2015, when I was at the peak of my mental illness struggles, she did something for me that I have treasured forever. She wrote me a bunch of letters and put them in envelopes for me to read later. She titled each one 'To open when you're feeling . . .' — things like 'alone' or 'overwhelmed'. In each envelope was a letter, a card with a quote on it, and photos of Cahlia and me together.

I held onto these letters tightly for the following year, reading over them many times, especially at 3 a.m. when my mind would begin to amp up. Her letter titled 'To open when you're feeling suicidal' was one that I clung onto the most. I put it in my bag and carried it with me pretty much everywhere. These letters were something that kept me going — something that enabled me to feel a little less alone and gave me the courage to fight when I needed it the most.

Today, one of the things I am asked most often when I am helping other people is if I can write them or their loved ones a letter to keep them going through their mental health struggles. Those frequent requests, along with those letters from Cahlia, gave me the inspiration to write you this book. It is filled with these kinds of letters — letters for you to read when you are feeling a certain way or experiencing something difficult.

I have asked a few trusted people in my world to also write letters, about things that I don't personally have experience of, or where I feel it might be helpful for you to hear from someone else. I have also partnered with an incredible psychologist, Dr Kirsten Davis from The Psychology Group, to ensure that there are some quick, practical tips from a professional spread throughout the letters.

This book is different from others in that it is not designed for you to read chronologically. The idea is for you to look through the titles, flick through and read whatever letter you need in that moment. It is divided into letters on emotions, experiences and beliefs. If you are unsure of where to start, try to identify the emotion that you are feeling (happiness, sadness, fear, etc.) and start there.

While I wish that I could write a letter for every experience possible, I simply couldn't, as that would be the world's longest book! However, these letters have all been asked for by people who follow me on social media, and I selected the most frequently requested ones to include.

There is also a section at the end of the book listing helplines and other support services, if you are in need of direct support. If you are in crisis or actively suicidal, then please call your local police or suicide hotline.

I know how difficult life can be, and how at times it feels like no one understands. I know there can be so much fear of asking for help, or even knowing where to turn or what to do. It is my hope that this little book helps you feel less alone.

You are not alone.

These are 'Letters to You'.

All my love,

Jazz

PART 1:

Emotions

To read when you are feeling angry

Dear you,

Anger is something that every single person will feel at different times during their life. The reasons why people feel angry, and the level at which they feel, differs from person to person, but the emotion itself is natural. We see this in kids as young as toddlers, when they throw temper tantrums! Anger is an important emotion, as it acts as a radar to show that something is wrong. It enables us to address injustice and, if we allow it, it can be an emotion that causes us to create change.

There have been many different experiences in my own life that have made me feel angry, and at times I didn't know how to regulate the intensity of my anger. I am by no means a professional, but what I have come to understand is that there are times when anger is absolutely appropriate, and other times when you may not even know why you feel angry or when your anger is seemingly misplaced.

For example, I get really angry when I see injustice in the

world, and that anger makes total sense. But there are also times that I have been angry at a person and then realised that they actually didn't do anything wrong and I was just responding out of my own fears, insecurities and misplaced hurt. Often it's not really about the emotion itself, but what we choose to do with it and how we choose to handle it.

While I don't know the reason for your anger, I do know some practical tools that can help manage the emotion and prevent it from causing damage.

One of the most important things I have learnt is to separate my emotions from my actions. It can be easy to act impulsively when we are angry, but in doing so we often eliminate the thought process that goes 'Is this what is best?' or 'Will this action help this situation?' Feeling the emotion of anger is OK, but acting out of anger can lead to things that we didn't intend to happen.

Instead of expressing that anger in the heat of the moment, try going for a run or some other form of exercise, or distract yourself by reading a book, doing some guided meditation or something else you enjoy, and then once you feel calmer, go back and make a decision about how you want to act. Taking a step back in this way creates a bit of a buffer that can help us respond from more of a rational mind than an impulsive one.

It is also really important to try to talk to someone about what has made you feel this way, if you can. Talking helps unscramble what is going on in your mind, and having the space to talk and express yourself can help de-escalate your emotions. Make sure it's someone that you feel safe with, who you can feel free to let it all out with. It may be a friend, family member, counsellor or even a helpline. When we don't talk about what's bothering us, our mind can blow things up even more while we try to figure it all out. Having someone there to listen and bounce ideas off can be really beneficial — in order to be heard, but also to help you figure out whether or not your response is rational.

If you are someone who experiences more long-term, deeper anger issues, then I really encourage you to try to seek out help from a professional. It might also be a good idea to create a list of things that you can do when you are feeling angry, to help you navigate it and ride through it. I personally have not dealt with long-term anger, but I know that so many people live with it and struggle with it immensely. To you I say that you are not alone and your identity is not in your anger.

I have seen lots of people feel really down and get angry at themselves because they know that they struggle with this and find it hard to stop it. Please know that there will be reasons that you respond and feel this way. Our human responses and behaviours are formed by different influences in life, and there may be some things that you need to unlearn and rebuild in healthy ways. The most important thing is both acknowledging it and then being brave enough to ask for help.

This emotion will pass. Sometimes it takes a little time and hard work, but you can overcome it.

You are not alone.

Breathe, ask for help, and keep fighting.

You've got this!

All my love,

Jazz

THIS emotion
WILL pass.

To read when you are feeling anxious

Hey!

I'm sorry to hear that you are feeling anxious right now. It isn't a nice feeling at all — I know from experience!

Maybe you are feeling anxious because of something that has happened, or might happen. Maybe you have no idea why you are feeling this way but are struggling to calm your mind. But the first thing I want you to know is that anxiety is temporary. This feeling will pass, so stay with me.

First, slow down your breathing. Try to breathe in while you count to four in your head, hold for seven, and then breathe out for eight. Focus on your breath and keep doing this until you are breathing slowly and calmly.

There is a really popular tool that I was taught for dealing with anxiety. It is called the 5, 4, 3, 2, 1 method, and I want you to give it a go with me.

First, notice five things that you can see.

Then four things that you can touch (one of them being this book!).

Three things that you can hear.
Two things you can smell.
One thing you can taste.

It might seem like a weird thing to ask you to do, but this tool can really help ground you and help your mind to know that right now, in this moment, you are safe. All you need to focus on is the present, and nothing else. You can't change what has happened, and you don't know the future. When you are feeling anxious, one of the best things you can do is simply be in the moment.

My friend Genevieve Mora, the co-founder of Voices of Hope, struggled a lot with anxiety as a teenager and has learnt a lot about it. I have asked her to write to you too, as someone who has lived through it herself and understands how you might be feeling.

Remember, your anxiety is not bigger than you. It will not take you out. You are strong, you are brave, you can do this. One minute at a time.

You have got this.

Jazz

HEY YOU,

I WANT TO START BY SAYING THAT ANXIETY IS SOMETHING I KNOW ALL TOO WELL. I REMEMBER FIRST FEELING ANXIOUS AT THE AGE OF TEN, AND TO THIS DAY IT'S STILL SOMETHING I EXPERIENCE, ALTHOUGH TO A MUCH LESSER DEGREE.

THAT FEELING IN THE PIT OF YOUR STOMACH, THE RUSH THAT GOES THROUGH YOUR BODY, YOUR MIND RACING A MILLION MILES AN HOUR, THE SWEATY PALMS, SHAKY LEGS ... I KNOW WHAT IT'S LIKE, SO LET ME START BY SAYING <u>YOU ARE NOT ALONE</u>.

I LEARNT A LOT THROUGH MY JOURNEY, AND I WOULD LOVE TO SHARE WITH YOU THE THINGS THAT HELPED ME THE MOST WHEN I WAS STRUGGLING, IN THE HOPE THAT THEY WILL HELP YOU TOO.

1. <u>POSITIVE MANTRAS</u>

I FOUND IT HELPFUL TO REPEAT THESE THINGS TO MYSELF IN MOMENTS OF ANGST.

* ANXIETY IS TEMPORARY
* IT CANNOT HURT ME
* THOUGHTS ARE NOT REALITY

I WOULD REPEAT THESE OVER AND OVER AGAIN IN ORDER TO CALM MYSELF DOWN.

2. <u>SHARING THE LOAD</u>

IN THE MOMENTS WHEN I WAS FEELING ANXIOUS, TELLING SOMEONE I TRUSTED HOW I WAS FEELING MEANT THAT I COULD BE SUPPORTED THROUGH THAT MOMENT. HAVING SOMEONE (IN MY CASE, USUALLY MY MUM) SIT

WITH ME AND ENCOURAGE ME TO USE MY COPING SKILLS MADE WHAT
SEEMED A SCARY SITUATION LESS SCARY.

3. 5-4-3-2-1
I TOTALLY AGREE WITH WHAT JAZZ SAID ABOVE – THIS IS A TECHNIQUE I
USED A LOT IN ORDER TO GROUND MYSELF AND HELP MYSELF FOCUS ON THE
PRESENT.

4. SIT WITH IT
I LEARNT THAT IN ORDER TO OVERCOME ANXIETY, I HAD TO FACE IT. THIS
MEANT SITTING WITH THAT UNCOMFORTABLE FEELING YOU AND I KNOW ALL
TOO WELL, UNTIL IT PASSED. THROUGH THIS PROCESS, I WAS REMINDED TIME
AND TIME AGAIN THAT IT ALWAYS _DOES_ PASS. SOMETIMES IT COULD TAKE A
LITTLE LONGER TO FADE, BUT IT ALWAYS DID. TRUST ME ON THIS.

YES, ANXIETY IS UNCOMFORTABLE TO FEEL AND EXPERIENCE, BUT I ALSO
KNOW THAT IT'S POSSIBLE TO GET THROUGH THESE MOMENTS AND YOU DO
TOO, BECAUSE YOU HAVE GOT THROUGH IT BEFORE.
  BE KIND TO YOURSELF. YOU WILL BE OK. BREATHE IN, BREATHE OUT.
  YOU'VE GOT THIS.
  GEN

One of the best things you can do is simply be in the moment.

ANXIETY – TIPS AND TOOLS

BY DR KIRSTEN DAVIS FROM THE PSYCHOLOGY GROUP

Here are some ideas for dealing with feelings of anxiety, which may help you feel more calm and able to cope.

DOES YOUR ANXIETY FIT THE FACTS?

Fear is an essential survival instinct. Anxiety evolved as a mechanism to keep us safe when there is danger that is causing a serious risk to our life, health or wellbeing. Our natural action urge is to fight the threat, to run away and avoid the danger, or to freeze. (This is known as the fight/flight response.)

The goal in managing anxiety is not always to get your emotional level down to zero. Instead, it is to *regulate* your emotion to a level that fits the facts of the situation. The experience of anxiety itself is not harmful . . . although it is unpleasant.

Ask yourself: right now, is my life in danger? Am I about to get injured or hurt? In almost all situations the answer is no.

The next step is to ask 'What is the threat?' Try to discover what might be causing you to feel anxious. Some examples include:

* lots of 'what if's
* worrying what others think of you
* predicting that bad things are going to happen
* ruminating over something that has already happened
* worrying about Covid-19
* uncertainty about the present or future
* fear of failure at school.

Some of the things that you are worrying about might make sense, but the *level* of anxiety you are feeling may be too high relative to the actual threat. So now you can work on reducing your anxiety to a level which is appropriate to the threat or stress you are facing.

ANCHOR YOUR CONSCIOUSNESS TO YOUR BREATH

When you are anxious, and your fight/flight response system is activated, your body prepares to protect itself by increasing your breathing and heart rate, and diverting blood flow to major muscle groups. Your breathing can become rapid and shallow, and you may gasp, sigh or hold your breath. This contributes to the physical sense of anxiety you are experiencing.

Check in with your breathing. If you are taking more than eight to twelve breaths per minute, you need to practise a breathing exercise. Aim to slow your breathing to about six breaths per minute (so one breath cycle, in and out, lasts ten to twelve seconds).

Place a hand on your stomach, between your ribs and belly button. Place your other hand on your chest, just below your collarbone.

Keep your shoulders and chest still and breathe in and out through your nose. Breathe right into your stomach and feel the rise and fall of your hand as you breathe in and out.

As you breathe, count slowly to ten — in for five, out for five. Repeat until your breathing is calm and slow.

CHALLENGE YOUR THOUGHTS
Ask yourself . . .

* Is this going to matter in a few minutes, a day or a week?
* What am I predicting might happen? Is there another possible outcome?
* If the worst happens, what could I do to cope with it? Could I live through it?
* What would I say to a friend in this situation?
* How could I think about this situation to make me feel better about it?

OTHER TIPS
Keep a notebook by your bed, and write down the thoughts that keep you awake. In the morning, go through and problem-solve what you can.

'Postpone' your anxiety — have a time of the day 'booked in' to do your worrying. If worry comes up earlier in the day, tell yourself you will have time for that later. When the time comes, you may find the worries have faded. Worry is often short-lived. And worry can be helpful — it is our brain's way of thinking through a problem.

Create distance between you and the thought in the very moment you notice it. Say 'I notice I'm having this thought' and let it pass.

To read when you are feeling guilty

Hey you,

I know that this feeling of guilt can seem like a really hard one to navigate at times. While I don't know the reasons or circumstances around why you feel this way, I want you to know your actions are not your identity and that we all mess up from time to time.

Guilt is a natural human emotion and response that we all feel at times. It is often an indicator that we have done something wrong, but when it comes to mental illness and the behaviours that can result from that, we can find ourselves experiencing a continuous feeling of guilt. Often this can escalate our behaviour and thoughts because the weight of guilt can feel so heavy.

For me personally, feelings of guilt were something that really dominated my life, and at times would even push me into crisis mode. For some of you that may seem odd that the feeling of guilt could push you into crisis, but many of you will understand exactly what I mean, because you too have experienced or are experiencing that. In my life it looked like this:

My mental illness would often see me behaving in unhealthy ways, and people would have to take me to the hospital or spend hours trying to counsel me through crisis moments. While these moments were so extremely hard, what I often found even harder was the aftermath, when I would feel so incredibly guilty that people had had to spend time taking me to the hospital or helping me when I knew they had busy lives. I felt guilty being in hospital, because I felt others with physical health needs deserved the bed. I felt guilty that I couldn't control my emotions and that I would act out in response to that. I also felt guilty about things that had happened to me, situations where my mind told me 'You should have known better' or 'Why didn't you say something earlier?' I also had 'survivor's guilt' after losing a friend to suicide who had a similar story to mine — a feeling of 'Why am I still here when she isn't?' All of this is to say that you are not alone in feeling this way.

Feelings of guilt can be triggered by so many different experiences and situations. My therapist and I were actually talking about this recently. I was explaining that even now I can still feel so guilty about my teenage years and my behaviours and responses, and the things I did that had hurt other people, and she said something to me that I had never heard before. She said, 'Jazz, every response and behaviour and emotion makes sense. It may not be the right behaviour or the best response, but something in your life has made you respond like that and so your behaviour in those moments, it makes sense.'

To give you a little more context on this, a specific example was that I felt a lot of guilt around the lengths that I would go to in order to avoid abandonment. Sometimes it would centre around me being in crisis, which always left me with this massive feeling of guilt and self-hatred for having acted that way. I didn't know why I was behaving like that, even when I knew that it was hurting people, and the guilt I carried around because of it became so heavy. However, my therapist pointed out that when I was three years old, my dad walked out on me and never came back, and so my little brain had started to fear being abandoned. I never learnt any tools for how to handle that, and as a teenager this self-destructive behaviour developed. While it wasn't the best or right response to my fear of abandonment, in my case it made sense.

Your behaviour, your responses, your emotions — they make sense, somehow. You don't have to try to dig up the reasons why, but you do need to show yourself a little bit of compassion.

If you can, try to talk to someone about how you are feeling (I highly recommend a professional, but also a friend or family member is good too!). Guilt is not something that you have to feel by yourself.

Sure, you may have messed up (we _all_ have at times), but you have to know that while you might make mistakes, _you_ are not a mistake. Your feelings of guilt do not encapsulate your identity. You can use this emotion to learn, grow and fight to change.

You have got this!

All my love,

Jazz

GUILT – TIPS AND TOOLS

BY DR KIRSTEN DAVIS FROM THE PSYCHOLOGY GROUP

1. Challenge your thinking — does your feeling of guilt make sense or fit the facts? Do you actually need to feel guilty?
2. Mindfully describe the situation to yourself (see page 217). What actually happened, and what did you do?
3. Think about the harm you caused, and consider what an appropriate repair would be. This could be a simple 'sorry', or you may need to go further than this, by showing you are sorry with your behaviour, not just words.
4. Be creative — there may be times when you don't have the opportunity to be able to repair the harm caused. What could you do instead? Maybe you could write a letter saying sorry even if that person can no longer receive it.
5. Regulating your feelings of guilt does not mean getting rid of them entirely. Experiencing some sense of guilt is helpful, as it makes us think twice about doing the same thing again.
6. Don't over-apologise. Make amends, and move on.
7. If your feelings of guilt do not fit the facts, then go back into the situation, talk to the person involved, don't hide.

To read when you are experiencing depression

Hey!

I am sorry that you are dealing with this at the moment. Depression can be so difficult, and often feels like you're walking through mud. I know that at times it can feel isolating, overwhelming and never-ending, but I want you to know that you are not alone, and that things can get better. For many people, depression can be a long-term battle, but it is possible for you to learn to manage it and still live a happy, healthy life.

I don't know what your situation is, or why you are struggling with this at the moment; if it is something that has been long term, or if you have been diagnosed with it recently. What I do know is that depression is not your identity — it is not your personality, or who you are. It is simply something that you are struggling with, which means that there is hope for change.

I know that I personally struggled for many years assuming that my mental illness was my identity — that it was just who I was, therefore it would never change. I stopped engaging in therapy or actively doing anything to help myself because I didn't see any point. Eventually I realised that actually my illness was <u>not</u> my identity, and this knowledge gave me a little more hope to fight and a little more hope for change.

There is no shame in having depression. It doesn't make you weak or worth any less, it is simply an illness that you are dealing with. And, like most illnesses, there are so many things that you can try to help you manage it.

I know that one of the most frustrating things is when people say things like 'just be happy', or hint that depression is a choice. It is <u>not</u> a choice, and I am so sorry for the number of times that you have probably heard that in your life. I know that it isn't easy, and I know that this battle feels long, draining and at times so isolating. But even in the midst of that isolating feeling, know that you are absolutely <u>not</u> alone — so many people fight and live with depression, people from sports stars to actors, CEOs, tradies, students . . . anyone. <u>You are not alone</u>.

One thing that I found helped me when I was struggling with depression was making an active choice to try to notice the good things in life. I would start and finish my day writing down three things that I was thankful for, which meant that throughout the day I was looking for even little things that I could write down at the end of it. Whether it be family, coffee, the sun . . . anything, big or small. Every day may not be good, but there is some good in every day. Cheesy, I know, but it's true! Sometimes you just have to be proactive in looking for it.

Another tool that I liked was learning to express myself creatively. Whether it be painting, drawing, writing, dancing, composing music, making things with clay . . . any way that you can express yourself. I tried painting once but I soon realised how terrible I was at it, and that my drawings looked like those of a three-year-old in kindergarten, so that wasn't for me! But I actually found a love for dancing. The physical side of it was good, but I began to learn contemporary, so I could also express myself through dance. I am not amazing at it, but it became a helpful and fun thing to do when I was feeling particularly low.

There are also the basic things, like exercising and eating well, that are really important in managing depression, and it is about finding what works for you. You don't have to try to force yourself to be happy, or fake your emotions to others — you just need to find things that can help relieve you and allow you to feel more at ease.

You are brave.

You are strong.

You are not alone.

Keep fighting, always.

So much love to you,

Jazz

EVERY DAY MAY NOT BE GOOD, BUT THERE IS SOME GOOD IN EVERY DAY.

To read when you are feeling sad

Hey you,

I'm sorry that you are feeling sad at the moment. Being sad can feel like a heavy weight.

There are many reasons and things in our lives that can make us experience this emotion — it is part of what makes us human! You might know what has made you feel sad — whether it is something that has happened, like a relationship breakdown, or a physical circumstance. Or you might have no idea why you are feeling sad. This happens, and it's OK.

Before I write more, I want you to know that even though I am going to give you a few practical tips that I use to help lift my mood, it is also really important to simply allow yourself to feel the emotion. You don't have to force yourself to try to feel happy, because that is not sustainable or healthy. I think that often we get caught in this societal idea that we don't want to 'bring the mood down', so we try to hide our feelings. Your feelings are valid, and it is OK to have the time, space and freedom to experience them. We then know what we can do to help ourselves move forward and not stay permanently in this emotion.

Each person responds to sadness differently, but there are a few things that have helped me when I have experienced it. One thing I started doing when I was feeling down was to start and finish every day by writing three things that I was thankful for. It could be things like 'I am thankful for coffee', or a person I was thankful for. At times it was the weather, a TV show, a moment that made me smile. Doing this both morning and night was strategically important for me, and I will tell you why.

Starting off your day thinking about three things you are thankful for means that you are setting yourself up with a mindset of gratitude. Even if you are in a difficult situation, it enables you to see a little light amongst it, knowing that you don't have to look too far to see small things that you are thankful for.

Then, finishing your day with another three things means that throughout the day you are almost looking for little (or big!) things that you can put on that list. It helps lift your spirit a tiny bit, and remind you that this emotion you are feeling right now won't last forever — that even when you feel bogged down with sadness, there are still small things in the world to look forward to that will bring you light.

It is important to try to find things that you enjoy doing. Maybe you could try writing a list of things that you can do when you are feeling down. Going for coffee with a friend, going to the beach or watching a comedy ('Brooklyn Nine-Nine' is my go-to fave!) are all little things that you can do to help lift your mood, even if only for a while.

I have also personally found that cleaning my bedroom is something that helps me when I am down — I think it's because my room often is a physical representation of where I am at, so when I am feeling down or stressed, then keeping my room tidy is often one of the first things to slip. Your physical environment can have an impact on your emotions, so if you are like me and things have maybe got a little messy, try to bring yourself to get up and clean up. Put on some music, clear out those dishes (I'm so bad at this) and get tidying!

If that isn't for you, you could also do things like paint or read, exercise or write — the list is endless and depends on what brings you even a little bit of joy. If you don't know what brings you joy yet, then this is the perfect opportunity to give some things a go.

Remember that it is OK to ask for help if you need it. Reach out to a friend or family member or anyone in your world that you trust, and let people walk this with you. You are not a burden. And if you have been feeling sad for an extended period of time, then please definitely do talk to someone, and even build up the courage to go and see your doctor to talk about it.

You don't have to do this alone.

It may feel stormy for you right now, but it won't be like this forever.

You've got this.

All my love,

Jazz

SADNESS – TIPS AND TOOLS

BY DR KIRSTEN DAVIS FROM THE PSYCHOLOGY GROUP

1. Acknowledge how your sadness is real, makes sense and fits the facts of your situation. Validation is an intentional practice, where you accept that your experience of sadness is understandable. This does not mean you have to like or agree with it. Being able to 'sit with' justified sadness is important.

2. Once you have identified your sadness, describe it mindfully. Notice your urges to act in a certain way (e.g. stay in bed, hide from friends) and validate your right to feel this way. You then can make the choice to do the following:

   a. Tolerate and mindfully move through your experience of sadness without changing it. Spending time alone and slowing down your life can create the space for you to figure out what you need to do next. Make sure you are not blocking out your feeling of sadness: relax your face, breathe slower, and release tension by tensing and relaxing your muscles.

b.   Change your experience of sadness by:
+   getting active and acting opposite to the urges (e.g. move your feet over the side of the bed and stand up; plan one or two activities you experience some enjoyment in; organise to have a coffee with a friend)
+   feeling another emotion (watch a funny YouTube clip, listen to upbeat music)
+   contributing compassionately to others (be kind, smile at someone you pass by, bake for someone)
+   distracting your mind with another activity
+   changing something in your environment (go outside, wear bright-coloured clothing, light a candle)
+   doing something you have been putting off (clean your bedroom, message someone you care about).

Note: Depression and sadness are different experiences and emotions. Sadness makes sense when you experience the loss of something you have, or something you anticipated having. It may be associated with negative thoughts about yourself. Depression is a more constant, enduring, low mood, with negative thoughts about yourself, the world and the future. However, feelings of sadness that last for days or weeks can lead to depression.

To read when you are having a good day

Hey friend!

I'm so glad that you are feeling happy today! That is so wonderful, I am literally smiling as I write this, knowing you are feeling this way.

To be able to feel joy, contentment or some peace about things is huge, and so incredibly important in our lives. You know what could be a really good thing to do right now? Pull out your journal, or even your phone, and write down three things that are making you feel happy. Is it friends? Family? Job? An animal? The weather? Write them down now and look back on them when you are having a not-so-good day. This can help remind you that the bad times don't last forever, and that while every day may not be good, there is good in every day.

You deserve to feel happy. You deserve to smile and laugh and to enjoy your day. To even, just for a moment, not feel the stress or other emotions of life and to simply be. What I think a lot of people don't understand is that someone who is struggling is not necessarily sad all the time. You can be struggling with your mental health and still have a good day; still experience joy and feel happy at times. Somehow we have skewed the idea that when someone is suffering, they must feel and look a certain way. I know for me, when I was in the midst of my battle, I still had good days, and at times I still felt happy. It doesn't make the struggle any less horrible, but it does provide a bit of relief.

Also, make sure you do your best to not self-sabotage this feeling. Sometimes when we don't think we deserve to feel happy, we can actively do things to take away the emotion, because we don't think we should be feeling that way — oh boy, was I good/terrible at that! If you know you do this, I want to remind you again and again that you deserve to feel happy — that it is a good thing and that it is an emotion that all humans should feel.

I even encourage you in this moment to think of how you might be able to make just one other person feel happy today, too. It might be as simple as smiling at someone on the street, sending a message or buying someone a coffee. Joy is contagious and right now, you have the ability to pass it on to others. And know that one day when you need it, others can pass it on to you.

You really do deserve every ounce of happiness you experience, and it is my hope that this feeling and emotion becomes even more prevalent in your life as you continue to grow and fight.

Now get out there and enjoy your day/night. Go for a walk, watch a movie, do things that make you feel happy — because you deserve it.

All my love,

Jazz.

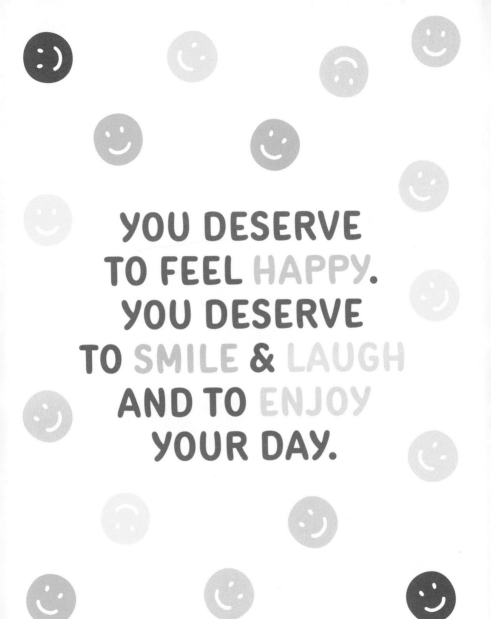

YOU DESERVE
TO FEEL HAPPY.
YOU DESERVE
TO SMILE & LAUGH
AND TO ENJOY
YOUR DAY.

To read when you are struggling with grief

Hi friend,

I am so sorry that you are going through this right now. Grief is such a hard, complex and overwhelming feeling. It is something that comes and goes throughout life, never fully leaving, and can be so incredibly painful.

I have experienced grief a lot in my own life, with the loss of many people, so I know how this feels. Grief can be experienced in so many different ways — that is just the nature of it. Anger, sadness, confusion, numbness, guilt . . . these are all things I have felt when dealing with grief. Whether it is over a recent loss, or one from years ago, grief is hard.

It has been six years since a friend of mine who I was mentoring, Jess, passed away. Some of you may have seen the series I made about her, called 'Jessica's Tree', where we told the story of her life to try to help others. I learnt a lot through the process of making that documentary, especially around my own grief process and my emotions around what happened.

There have been countless nights where I have just cried and cried. I got angry, I screamed, I went numb, I felt overwhelmed with sadness. I asked myself lots of questions: 'What if I had done this differently?' or 'What if I'd said this?' For the first couple of years these feelings struck me all the time, but eventually they became less frequent. I still feel them — I still have nights where I cry or moments where I feel angry that she isn't still here — but that is all a part of the process.

One of the hardest things that I faced during this time was the feeling of guilt. One of the biggest questions that comes with a sense of guilt is 'What if . . . ?' It can often become one of the biggest occupiers of our minds as we try to make sense of what happened and how we could have prevented it.

But these questions are normal, and they make sense. For a long time I thought that I was the only one who felt this way, and who felt the guilt of the outcome not being different. However, as I worked on 'Jessica's Tree' and got to talk in detail with many people in Jess's life, I began to realise that this was something that every single person was going through. Everyone was wondering what they could have said differently, or thought that if they had acted differently or responded differently or faster, Jess might still be here. So remember, you are not alone in feeling or thinking this way — but it is <u>so</u> important that you talk to someone about it.

If there was one thing that I wish I had known at the start it would be that it is a really good idea to see a counsellor to talk about what is going on. They can give you the space to ask the questions, express the anger, feel the sadness and, most importantly, get the tools to help you manage it.

Grief is something that no human should have to go through, but something that we unfortunately all experience at some stage. It is one of those things that no matter how much you read about it, nothing can really prepare you for it — the whirlwind of emotions that you experience and everything else that comes with it.

Try not to be too hard on yourself, and don't hold yourself to any idea of what grief should look or feel like. Everyone responds differently to it, but what I want you to know is that you are not alone.

It is OK to feel angry.
It is OK to feel sad.
It is OK to feel confused.
It is OK to feel overwhelmed.

It is OK to ask for help.
It is OK to talk to people.

You are not alone.

All my love,
Jazz

Don't hold yourself
to any idea of what grief
should look or feel like.

PART 2:

Experiences

To read when you are feeling alone

Hello you!

I am sorry that you are feeling this way right now. Humans are created for connection and relationship, and to feel alone is really difficult.

Let me start by saying that even though it feels like it, you are not alone. There are many people who have been where you are right now and who have fought through to the other side. I am here, in this book, with you. In fact, this whole book was written to ensure that no matter how you are feeling in these moments, you are never alone.

I personally have battled feeling alone for a lot of my life. It is something that I constantly had to fight, and had to be so intentional about fighting. What I know to be true is that even though in this exact moment it might feel like you are completely alone, you have people who love you, and there are people who can help you.

I remember getting myself into this pattern of feeling alone, when I would start to push people away or isolate myself. Because I left home at the age of 16 and began to fend for myself, I became very independent and slipped into the mindset of 'I don't need people, I will do this by myself. I can look after myself.' I guess learning to pay bills and rent and becoming my own independent guardian at such a young age encouraged me to feel this way! But while my situation definitely made me feel alone, looking back I realise that there was <u>always</u> someone there, whether it was a teacher, a counsellor, a friend or a helpline. So if right now you are feeling like you physically don't have anyone, remember that there are always people out there who you can talk to.

But feeling alone doesn't always mean physically being alone — I know this for sure. If you are battling mental illness or mental distress, sometimes you can feel the most isolated when you are surrounded by people.

I remember once when I was feeling particularly low, I was attending a conference at Spark Arena in Auckland. There were thousands of people there, including a lot of my friends. But I remember walking into the huge room, seeing it flooded with people and feeling so incredibly alone. I thought, 'I am sitting here with all of these people, but no one knows how I am feeling.' I was afraid of how people would respond if they knew what I was struggling with, or that if I tried to explain it to them, they wouldn't understand.

If that is how you are feeling, then I encourage you to try to write a letter to someone who you trust, explaining this.

I personally have found writing letters really helpful. I know that it can be really hard to articulate your feelings when you are face to face with someone. Words can get jumbled, and we begin to over-think and then we walk away, thinking of everything that we wish we had said. Taking time to write a letter expressing how you are feeling can be a really great way to open the conversation and let someone in.

Feeling like you are alone can be confusing. You might have family or friends, and know that you have people in your world who care about you, yet still feel alone. That could be because you don't feel understood, or people don't know what you are fighting, or you feel as though you are the only one going through this. It may be that you haven't shared your struggles with people, or maybe you have and it wasn't well received. Either way, you are not doing this alone. You are not fighting this by yourself.

A friend of mine recently was talking about a report that had been done on the 'epidemic of loneliness'. A large study has been done into loneliness and what it actually means for people. They managed to narrow it down to three types of loneliness:

1. Intimate. Missing a connection with a trusted confidant. This could be a partner or best friend, or anyone who you don't feel you have to put up a façade for.

2. Relational. Missing having friends — engaging in social

activities, hanging out with people and going on walks or to the movies. Late-night car-ride kinda vibes.

3. Collective. This one is all about wanting to feel like you are a part of something bigger than yourself — a community of people with a similar purpose and shared identity.

You could have an amazing family, but maybe you don't have great friends. Or maybe you don't have a community or feel like you know people who have a similar purpose to you. It only takes something to be missing in one of these areas for you to feel alone.

For me personally, I really struggled with intimate loneliness. I had friends and I had a community, but I didn't have close family. I often felt so alone when push came to shove, and I would avoid events like Christmas and birthdays because of the loneliness I felt at those times. However, that gap was filled for me by my new 'adopted' family, who chose to treat me as one of their own and became the people that I could be completely and utterly myself with.

I think that living through the Covid pandemic has amplified this feeling of being alone — for some who have never felt it before, and for others who found it to be a physical representation of what they already feel mentally. As a society, when we went into lockdown, each of us experienced this differently but the general concept was the same:

physical isolation. I was doing a lot of media interviews during this time about how people could stay connected even when they were physically isolated — things like regular Zoom calls with friends or picking one person every day to message, to keep up a sense of connection. I feel these tools are relevant not only in a pandemic, but also for any person who is feeling the weight of loneliness.

To you I simply say: you are not alone. You were never designed to do life alone. You have people cheering you on every step of the way. I am cheering you on. I am in your corner, and so are so many other people. Know that I, and other mental health advocates, do all that we do for you — so that you will know that there is hope, and you don't have to fight this alone.

I encourage you to reach out to someone as soon as you finish this letter: a teacher, counsellor, family member, friend or a helpline — someone in your immediate world who can listen to you and support you.

You are not alone.

All my love,

Jazz

FEELING ALONE – TIPS AND TOOLS

BY DR KIRSTEN DAVIS FROM THE PSYCHOLOGY GROUP

1. Build a sense of connection — with people, animals, nature, the world.
2. Go outside with bare feet. Experience the feeling of your feet on the ground and your connection to the earth.
3. Exercise more often. Consider how to broaden your social network through exercise. Go to the gym, do a class at a yoga studio or join a sports club or team. You may meet people with similar interests. If that feels too much, then maybe start with a walk around the block, giving a gentle smile to those you pass.
4. Connect with a pet. Spend time with your pet. Pay close attention to the feel of their fur and their warmth as you cuddle or pat them. If you don't have a pet, talk to someone you know who has a pet, and offer to take it for a walk or look after it.
5. Find a group of people with whom you have similar interests. Join a club in person or meet up online.

To read when you are feeling stressed

Hello!

You're feeling stressed, hey? This is a totally normal and human feeling, but knowing that it's 'normal' doesn't minimise what you are experiencing right now.

We all have to deal with stress — it is something that I often feel, especially with my workload (I have most definitely felt this over the last couple of months, while I have been writing this book!). Stress is our body's response to challenges or demands, mental or physical. In short bursts, it can be positive, and encourage us to take action to avoid danger or get something done. There are so many things that can cause us to feel this way: school, exams, work deadlines, relationships, finances, having too many things to do and not enough hours in the day. The list goes on and on!

Although right now it might feel overwhelming, know that this feeling isn't going to last forever, and there are things that you can do in this moment to help bring a little bit of clarity to your mind and let you make a plan to deal with it.

When I was in the middle of directing my first show, 'Jessica's Tree', my stress levels were really high. I was having to hit multiple deadlines, putting pressure on myself and juggling everything else in life. I remember saying to someone that I felt so stressed and I didn't know if I could handle it. This person said to me: 'No, Jazz, you <u>can</u> handle it — you just need help. And you need to ensure that you are doing basic self-care things, despite the deadlines.'

Those were wise words. I think we can all be guilty of letting basic self-care slip when we are in a busy season — I will be the first to admit that I can be terrible at that! However, I am learning the importance of always making time for self-care — things like exercising, sleeping, and eating healthily — because in some situations, it can prevent me getting to the point of being overwhelmed by stress. (By the way, if you are feeling like you are already at the point of being totally overwhelmed, then flick to my letter on page 64 'to read when feeling overwhelmed' — it will help you in this moment.)

For me, the first thing to slip was exercise. (Now, I know that some of you reading this book will have a personal struggle with exercise, as part of your issues around food. If that is you, then you can skip the next couple of paragraphs. By the way, I have had a friend of mine who has been in your position write a letter just for you — read the rest of the tips below and turn to page 100 to read how to manage that!) I simply wasn't making time to exercise. At all. I am usually pretty good at going to the gym or going for regular walks with friends, but when the deadlines hit I stopped and focused on the work.

However, there is so much evidence that suggests that exercise is hands down one of the most important things you can do to help relieve stress. I don't know quite how it works, but researchers say that putting stress on your physical body can help lessen your mental stress.

This looks so different for everyone, so it is important to see what works for you and begin to incorporate it in your routine. For a lot of people this can be going for a walk every day — getting outside, getting some fresh air and walking is so good for your mind and body. For me, however, I don't enjoy walking for exercise unless I am doing it with friends. Instead, I love to do short, high-intensity classes at the gym (boxing is my fave!). I am in and out within thirty minutes, and I always feel mentally clearer and filled with endorphins afterwards. Some people like doing dance classes, going on a tramp, running, swimming, playing sports . . . Basically, all of this is to say <u>don't neglect exercise</u>, as it is a very simple thing that helps with stress management. In fact, why don't you go for a walk, hit the gym, dance or do something <u>today</u> to help with what you are feeling right now?

Now this next one may be hard for you to hear . . . but when you are dealing with stress you should try to <u>reduce</u> your caffeine intake, not increase it. I became an avid coffee drinker about seven years ago and it quickly became associated in my brain as coffee = work. Drink more coffee to stay awake and do more work. But the extra caffeine is not doing your stress levels any good. So if you are cramming for exams or a test, or trying to get through a massive workload, <u>slow down on the coffee</u>. Drinking too much of it can cause anxiety and add to the stress. Swap it out for decaf, a smoothie or even water.

My next tip: write out everything that you need to do onto paper — all of it. Get everything out. Then go through and number each thing in order of importance, from highest to lowest. Sometimes getting it all out and seeing it on paper can help unscatter the brain a little bit. Push everything in the lowest category to one side and focus on only the three most important things. Of those three, which one has the closest deadline or is the absolute priority? Do that one first, and make a plan for when you can work on the rest.

Another thing that might help is something I have started doing recently — sectioning my days into six parts:

Morning routine (shower, breakfast, journal, etc.)
Morning work block
Lunch
Afternoon work block
Dinner
Evening block

Then I can look at what I have to do for the week, colour-code all of my tasks into themes or categories, and put them into my calendar to make sure that I have dedicated enough time to work on all of them.

If your feeling of stress has to do with relationships, then make sure you talk with someone that you trust. Try writing a letter describing everything that you are feeling, and then think about what the next step might be to resolve the situation and reduce your stress.

The most important thing for you to know right now is that this feeling will pass. It is not permanent, and you _will_ be OK. I know that it can feel so huge, but remember to take a step back and know that in the grand scheme of life, this is one moment. Your wellbeing is the top priority — and being the best version of yourself means that you will be able to do your tasks to the best of your ability.

You've got this!

Breathe, slow it down, you will be OK.

All my love,

Jazz

Breathe, slow it down.

To read when you are feeling overwhelmed

Hey you!

First of all, breathe. The feeling of being overwhelmed can almost seem paralysing — and I know that feeling too. Feeling overwhelmed is something that every human experiences from time to time. It can be due to many different reasons or situations in your life — whether it be from saying yes to too many tasks, then having too much to do and not knowing where to start and so not doing any of them at all and procrastinating (that's me!), or because waves of emotions are causing you to feel overwhelmed.

Either way, you are not alone in this.

For me personally, this feeling comes up often. The ways in which it is expressed, and the reasons for it, have changed throughout the years, but the baseline feeling remains the same. For many years, it was emotions that would overwhelm me — emotions that I didn't know how to articulate, express or even understand. I felt like life was hitting me all at once and that my emotional cup was constantly overflowing.

It can feel really difficult to regulate these emotions, but there is a lot of help out there, especially things like CBT (cognitive behavioural therapy, which helps you change your thinking in order to change your behaviour) and DBT (dialectical behavioural therapy, which is a type of CBT that combines strategies like mindfulness, acceptance and emotion regulation), that can help you manage and navigate what to do with the overwhelming emotions. If this is something you feel often, then don't be afraid to seek out professional help from a counsellor, because they can teach you techniques and strategies to help you in these moments.

I may be a mental health advocate but I too still get emotionally overwhelmed at times! It's OK — it is totally human and normal! There have been a huge number of times that I have felt crippled by the feeling, or spent the night crying at a friend's house, feeling stuck. It happens, but the important thing is that there are tools that we can use in this moment to help us get through it.

There are a lot of practical things that you can do when you are feeling overwhelmed. You could probably spend hours scrolling the internet to find solutions — but I am going to give you a few main ones that really help me when I am feeling this way. Then on page 70 you will find some quick tips from our psychologist, too!

1. GET UP AND PHYSICALLY GO FOR A WALK

I know that walking doesn't take away the worries of the world, but it can take you away from your worries for a moment. The act of taking yourself out and physically creating space to try to quieten your mind can really help. It enables you to put space between you and the things that are making you feel overwhelmed.

As you walk, put on some music, or if that still makes you think too much, chuck on a podcast or listen to an audio book. Podcasts are really great because you have to actively listen to them, meaning that there is less chance for your mind to start wandering and over-thinking again.

When you have time, write a list of some good recommended podcasts and playlists so that you have some 'go-tos' stored in your phone, rather than furiously trying to research and hunt for one when you are already feeling overwhelmed!

Podcasts and audio books are also a really good go-to in general to help focus your mind. I often listen to them while driving or as a way to get off social media. I can potter around while listening.

2. WRITE DOWN THE THINGS THAT ARE OVERWHELMING YOU

Whether it be emotional or situational, writing things out on paper is a great way to declutter the mind. It doesn't have to be well thought out or articulated well. Just 'word vomit' on a page and write everything you are feeling. There is something about getting what is in your mind out on paper that can help it feel a little clearer. It can also be a good reminder that you have got through this kind of emotion before, and you can do it again.

For those of you who may find this triggering, and might find yourself re-reading it over and over again, I understand. I struggled with that for a long time. What I found helpful was getting it all out, and then ripping up the pages. There are some journals I have from back in my teenage years which are cool to look back on to see how far I have come, but I actually threw a lot of them out as I went through the motions, and that is more than OK too! What is important right now is that you feel able to get it all out.

When I am feeling this way now or am really struggling with my emotions, I will write it all out on my iPad and then erase it. It actually feels so good to literally wipe the slate clean!

3. READ
Off the back of that, reading is a great tool to slow down the mind and to allow you to escape your current reality for a while. Reading forces your mind to slow down (which, if it is anything like my speedy mind, it is necessary to do often). Grab your favourite book, put your phone away, find yourself a nice place to sit and read. Even 15-20 minutes can do wonders.

Reading isn't for everyone (I know this, as sometimes I struggle to do it myself as my mind wanders off the pages!), but what I find really helpful is to listen to the audio book while reading along. It can help keep your mind focused on what you are reading, rather than letting it drift off back into the overwhelming feelings.

4. MEDITATION

Meditation isn't for everyone either. I personally don't do it a lot, but I know that it is something that so many people find so beneficial. I should probably do more of it! Being able to slow down your mind and focus on the moment in front of you right now allows you to really stabilise and ground yourself and be present in the moment. Controlling your breathing and slowing down your thoughts is so beneficial to your wellbeing.

5. ASK FOR HELP

Remember, you are not in this alone. It is OK to pick up the phone and talk to someone. You don't even have to tell them everything if you don't want to. Getting out and being with people, going for a walk or just hanging out, can really help. I will often ask one of my friends to grab a coffee (decaf if I'm jittery!) and walk in the park. It's a way to take my mind off my chaotic emotions and slow down a little.

It is also really beneficial to talk with someone about what you are feeling — a family member, friend, teacher, work

colleague or even a helpline. (A therapist is my new fave —
they really help with these feelings, too!) You don't have
to fight these thoughts yourself, and often it can take an
external perspective for you to step outside of yourself and
know that you are going to be OK.

These are all great things to do when you are feeling
overwhelmed <u>and</u> great things to do often as a preventative
to feeling this way. I couldn't tell you the number of times I
would let all of these things slip, thinking that I was OK, and
then eventually I would start feeling really overwhelmed again
and thinking 'How did I even get here!?'

Make time for the little things that help you keep on
top of your own mental wellbeing. <u>You</u> are the priority —
everything else can wait.

This feeling will pass. You are going to be OK. Slow it down,
breathe. You have got this.

All my love,

Jazz

FEELING OVERWHELMED – TIPS AND TOOLS

BY DR KIRSTEN DAVIS FROM THE PSYCHOLOGY GROUP

Emotional overwhelm is the experience of intense emotions that are difficult to manage. When an emotion is triggered, we often feel gripped by it and it limits our ability to think clearly and choose how we want to respond. As time passes, and with awareness, we can pause and have a clearer mind to be able to make a thoughtful choice about how we respond.

Emotions are normal. We need to learn to accept them, express them, validate them and learn from them. The end goal is that they are effective . . . not always comfortable. People often overestimate the duration of strong feelings. Riding the wave of emotion is challenging, however there is a middle, and they do pass. Here are a few tips and tools to help when you feel overwhelmed:

1. Mindfully observe and describe what you are feeling. Notice what is going on inside and outside of you. What is the situation? What are your thoughts/feelings? What are others doing?

2. Using the signature of emotions chart (see page 203), can you identify what emotions you are feeling? The first step to changing

an emotion is to identify it and how you experience it in terms of physical sensations, action urges, actions and thoughts. The next step is to decide whether or not the emotion, and its intensity, fits the facts, and adjust it if necessary (see page 205).

3. What is causing you to feel overwhelmed? Is it a situation, something that happened, or your own thoughts? Write it down and/or talk it through with a friend or family member.

4. Are there particular problems you can solve that will make you feel less overwhelmed? If yes, think of one at a time and brainstorm some solutions. Then take the next steps to solve it.

5. If you can't solve the problem/s:
    + be mindful in the moment. Stay present by choosing an object and describing it in detail (the colour, texture, size, weight and anything else you notice)
    + tolerate the emotion. Experience it without acting on it, and 'surf' its ebb and flow. Remind yourself 'this too shall pass'
    + practise radical acceptance (see page 215)
    + distract your mind until you can solve the problem
    + remember you are 'stuck' not 'broken'
    + do something you enjoy until you feel more calm.

To read when you are having suicidal thoughts

Dear you,

BEFORE I START THIS LETTER, I WANT TO SAY THAT IF YOU FEEL THAT YOU ARE AT RISK OF HURTING YOURSELF RIGHT NOW, THEN PLEASE CALL EITHER A MENTAL HEALTH CRISIS NUMBER, OR THE POLICE. (THERE IS A LIST OF HELPLINES AND NUMBERS AT THE END OF THIS BOOK, ON PAGE 198.) YOU MAY FEEL ALONE AND LIKE IT'S IMPOSSIBLE, BUT THERE ARE PEOPLE WHO CAN HELP YOU.

THERE IS ALSO ANOTHER LETTER IN THIS BOOK TITLED 'TO READ WHEN YOU ARE FEELING ACTIVELY SUICIDAL' — IF YOU ARE FEELING LIKE YOU WANT TO ACT ON THESE THOUGHTS AT THE MOMENT, THEN TURN OVER TO THAT LETTER ON PAGE 82.

First of all, I am so sorry that you are feeling in a way that brought you to this letter. You are so needed in this world. You may not feel it right now, but there is only one of you and no one could ever fill that gap. You are important, you are wanted, you are not a burden and the world is better with you in it.

I know this because I myself have felt this way before —
many times, in fact. If you know my story, then you will
know that I tried to take my own life multiple times, so I
understand the depth of what you may be feeling. While
every person's reasons for feeling this way are different, the
emotions and anguish are often similar.

I know for me, at times I felt suicidal because of external
situations — bullying, abuse, financial worries, relationship
breakdowns — and then there were many times that these
feelings came from my own perception of myself: thinking
that I was unlovable, that I was a burden to everyone around
me, and wholeheartedly believing that the world would be
better without me in it. I would feel myself responding in
ways that would push others away or hurt them. I would spend
hours looking in the mirror just wishing I could be someone else
— someone normal.

While these emotions, experiences and feelings were
overwhelming and very valid, I don't think I fully wanted to
die — I just wanted the pain to stop. Dying just felt like the
only option for me, because I felt as if I had exhausted all
other ways to stop feeling like this.

The reason I can confidently say that I didn't want to
actually die was that I knew that if someone could wave a
magic wand and suddenly everything would be different, then
I would be OK with living. But obviously that is not reality.
However, while we may not have a magic wand, what I have

come to understand is that often, time is that wand. Time helps heal. Time can eventually see us living a life we never thought possible.

Time can see our lives completely turn around. It can have us living in different countries, enjoying new careers, building new families or very simply just enjoying life. Time gives us space to heal, opportunities to unlearn old responses and relearn new ones. It can take you from believing that suicide is your only option to being thankful that you chose to stay.

It has been six years since my final suicide attempt, and I am living a life that I could have only ever dreamed of as I sat in a psych ward. A life that I could never have even comprehended — one that seemed impossible, to the point that I would never have even entertained the idea, because it seemed like something you would see in a movie. I have had the opportunity to travel the world — I have stood next to giraffes, climbed the Empire State Building and had dinner at Kensington Palace. I have watched sunsets in Bali and eaten croissants in Paris, all things that I absolutely never thought would be possible in my life. I came from poverty and couldn't even imagine getting on a plane. However, I am so thankful that I stuck around long enough to be able to see the world.

I have entered into my dream career of making film and TV and written books and spoken to audiences around the world. Above all of these things, however, what I am most thankful for is that I have learnt what family and unconditional love are. I have laughed till I cried with my friends, learnt what it is to 'do life' with other people and to feel a part of something greater than myself. I got to be here to understand that I am in fact more than the things that have happened to me, and that everything that I was going through would one day be a part of helping someone else. I love the quote 'Your story will be someone else's survival guide'. One day, you too could help other people.

I do not tell you this to say 'hey, look at my life' — because, trust me, among the 'success' is still a very chaotic life filled with emotions, challenges and learnings. I tell you this so that when you read the next words that I am about to say, you can read them knowing that there is hope.

And so to you, brave soul . . .

Keep fighting. Keep going. I know that right now in this moment it may seem impossible. It may feel like the world is crashing in around you. I don't know if it is situational, emotional, self-beliefs or anything else that are making you feel this way, but what I do know without a doubt is that the world needs you. <u>We</u> need you. Those who your story will impact in five years need you. Your family needs you. Your future family, wife, husband, kids, and grandkids need you.

You may not see it right now, but with time, you will. You are not the things that have happened to you, you are not the words that others have spoken over you. It doesn't matter what you have done, you are deserving of love and you deserve to be here. You deserve to be on this planet.

I know that feeling suicidal is one of the most debilitating and often all-consuming, dark experiences a person can have. It is human instinct to fight for survival, and to have a brain that is trying so hard to fight in the opposite direction is a tiring battle. I couldn't count the number of nights that I spent bawling my eyes out, experiencing the heartache, the overwhelming emotions. The feelings of numbness, of not caring anymore or losing interest in things you once loved. I understand those feelings, and I am writing this for you to know that even if you are experiencing all of those, hope is still real and change is still possible.

You are not too far gone. Your situation is not too messy. You are not a lost cause. You are a warrior, you are a fighter — and right now, you gotta start fighting. Not for me, but for you. Simply because you are worth it.

If you act on your thoughts now, you will never know what tomorrow might bring. You will never know what you might be doing in five years, ten years . . . the kids and grandkids that you may have had . . . the sunsets, weddings, celebrations . . . the adventures, the laughs, the careers. Pain will always be a part of life — no person is immune to it. However, with time, the way in which you respond to pain will change. You will grow.

You are worth it. If this entire book was created purely for <u>you</u> to choose to stay, then it is worth it, and I would do it a million times over. Because you are meant to be here. The world is better with you in it.

I know you may be thinking 'Jazz, you don't know me. You don't know what's happened to me or what I have done.' And you are right, I don't know. But what I do know is that you are still worth fighting for. You, as you are right now, are good enough. You are good enough.

Don't think that my story is an exception to the rule, or look at it thinking 'I could never do that'. I am by no means anything special or an exception. I simply learnt to fight, and with time I discovered my purpose.

Your purpose doesn't need to look the same as mine; it may be in teaching, counselling, business, sports — anything that you want. And while our purposes may be different, our worth is the same. If you feel like your situation is too big or like it could never turn around, then read the next letter (on page 82), where I will tell you a little bit more about my story in the hope that you will understand that anything can be turned around.

The next part of this book is very simply 50 reasons you should stay. Turn the page — let's remind you why life can be so beautiful amongst the chaos and pain.

Now, pick up your phone and message or call someone and let them know how you are feeling. I know that can feel scary and you don't want to burden someone with it. Maybe you feel like people won't understand, or maybe you feel like they are too busy, or have other priorities. But if there is anything I have learnt, it is that people would rather have you alive and messy than not here at all.

There is a list of helplines at the end of this book (see page 198) if you are struggling to know where to find support.

Take the step. Reach out.

You got this.

I believe in you.

All my love,

Jazz

50 REASONS TO STAY

1. Sunsets
2. Coffee dates with friends
3. Travelling the world
4. Meeting new people
5. Chilling on the beach at 3 a.m. with your friends
6. You are someone else's reason to stay
7. You haven't met everyone who is going to love you yet
8. Cupcakes
9. Sunrises
10. Learning new skills
11. Animals
12. Your favourite artist's new album
13. Snow fights
14. Warm showers on cold days
15. The smell of freshly mowed grass
16. To try every flavour of ice cream
17. To meet your future kids and grandkids
18. Graduation
19. Love
20. Getting your dream job one day

21. You will be someone else's reason to stay in the future
22. Writing a book
23. All the new TV shows and movies that are yet to come out
24. Hiking with friends
25. Picnics
26. Belly laughs
27. To watch your siblings, nieces, nephews or others grow up
28. To attend your best friend's wedding
29. Beach days
30. Hiring a kayak and going out at sunset
31. Laugh-till-you-cry moments
32. To pet all the dogs
33. The feeling of the sun and the breeze on your skin
34. Fluffy sweaters
35. Going to university or tech
36. Having your own family
37. The feeling you get when the kid in the room chooses to go to you out of everyone
38. Flowers
39. Finding the perfect iced coffee
40. Tasting new food
41. The moments where you just smile to yourself
42. Hugs
43. Creating your own bucket list
44. Seeing your favourite artist live
45. Learning to surf, paint, sew or knit

46. Dancing in the rain

47. Spontaneous adventures with friends

48. Seeing the seven wonders of the world

49. To hear the words 'I love you' and know they mean it

50. Because *you* are *worth it*!

To read when you are feeling actively suicidal

Hi friend,

First and foremost, the world needs you here. Thank you for turning to this letter instead of running directly with your thoughts right now. I want you to give me the next few minutes to talk to you — I need you to stay with me through this one, OK?

YOU MAY KNOW THE DRILL — IF YOU FEEL THAT YOU ARE AT IMMEDIATE RISK OF TAKING YOUR OWN LIFE, CALL THE POLICE OR A HELPLINE. IF YOU FEEL LIKE YOU CAN DO THAT IN THIS MOMENT, THEN PLEASE DO. IF NOT, KEEP READING AND HOPEFULLY BY THE END OF THIS LETTER YOU MIGHT FEEL ABLE TO ASK FOR HELP.

I don't know what in your life has happened for you to reach this point, but I know the feeling. I know the feeling of thinking that life just can't get better. The feeling that everyone will be better without you. The feeling of overwhelming pain or, perhaps, complete numbness.

I know the feeling, but I also know that as much as it

seems like it right now, these feelings will not last forever. This urge will pass. I am not saying that you will wake up tomorrow and your life will be great, but what I am saying is that this strong emotion and the feelings you have right now to act on your suicidal thoughts — it will pass.

I don't know if you know this, but one researcher has estimated that the actual chances of <u>you</u> existing are 1 in $10^{2,685,000}$ — or 10 followed by 2,685,000 zeros! The chances that you are on this planet right now and that you as a human being exist are an absolute miracle. You were not a mistake — you are here. You are that miracle.

You are so worth fighting for. And I am so sorry for every time that you have felt like you weren't worth it — when people or systems or maybe even professionals have made you feel like you are not enough, or that you are not worth fighting for. That is simply not true. In fact, I am writing this entire book with <u>you</u> in mind. I know I don't know you personally, but that doesn't mean that I don't care. I care deeply. I care because I know these feelings. I care because I have seen the aftermath of when someone does go through with it. I care because I know there is hope for you. I care because you are simply worth it. And there will be other people in your world who feel the same. <u>You are not alone</u>.

In one year, five years, ten years, your life could look completely different. You could be living in a totally different city. Maybe you will have kids or grandkids. You might study, get a different job, find a lover, discover many different passions — all things that you will never achieve if you leave us today.

Look at my own life, for example. I spent most of my teenage years believing wholeheartedly that the world was better off without me. I couldn't hold down a stable job or relationship. I grew up very poor, and carried that with me into my teenage years, when I lived off a benefit, in significant debt and unable to pay rent a lot of the time. I often didn't have money for food, and at times I even stole to survive. This was my life for many years. The only time I made ends meet was for one year while I worked at a gym, and then I went back into being broke, on a benefit and in debt. I grew up in poverty, I lived in poverty — I didn't know any other lifestyle.

I am now 26, and the last couple of years have been the first time in my life when I have finally become financially stable. I would never have thought it was possible to get to this point, but I am so glad that I stuck around, and that now not only do I not have to stress about being able to pay the rent but I can give to others.

Life can and _will_ change. That is the nature of life, and the power of time. If you told the girl once sitting exactly where you are right now that in a mere few years she would be an award-winning TV director, author and advocate, she would have laughed in your face. And let me tell you, I am not an exception to the rule. It is possible for your life to change — you just need to stick around long enough to see it.

And you know what? More than these physical things in my life changing, the biggest thing that has changed is that I have found happiness. I found family. I found trust in friendships and began to unlearn my beliefs that told me that I was a burden to other people. I began to understand that the people in my life today are not the people who hurt me in the past, and eventually I found community. These are all things that I would have missed had I not been here. In fact, this entire book would not exist if I had done what you are thinking of doing right now. Imagine the people's lives you could impact on the other side of your decision to stay?

A lot of people will say suicide is selfish, and that one of the reasons you should stay is other people. While the people who know you and care about you are 100 per cent a reason to stay (and I have seen the ripple effect of suicide, affecting other people, and how heart-wrenching it is not just for a moment, but for life for these people), more than others, <u>you</u> are the reason to stay.

The world needs <u>you</u>. You are not the negative things that people have said about you, over you or to you. You are not the actions of others — you are not even the actions and behaviours of yourself. These things are just responses to trauma or events in your life and have become your way of coping.

You are not a burden
You are not unlovable
You are not too far gone
You are not a mistake
You are not attention-seeking
You are not wasting people's time

You are worthy
You are loved
You are wanted
You are deserving
You are brave
You are <u>enough</u>.

There is so much that I want to say to you, but right now in this moment I ask you to do the most courageous thing that anyone in your position could do, and that is to ask for help. I know it can feel scary — for those who have been in this position before, I know you may fear being called an attention-seeker, or you may fear the process that will follow once you ask for help — but I am telling you right now that you are worthy of help.

If you have never felt like actually wanting to act on your thoughts before, then for you, too, asking for help right now in this moment is the bravest and best thing that you can do.

Asking for help does not make you weak — it makes you courageous.

I'm not going to lie: I am sobbing as I write this letter, thinking of those who are reading it — who are in a place where they feel they need to read it. <u>I see you</u>. I know you are in pain — but please, do not give up. The world needs you in it. We need you here. You deserve to be here. There is only one of you in this world — please don't give up today.

You have made it this far. You have made it through the last couple of minutes. Let's make it through tonight, OK? Make that call — let someone in. A friend, family member, professional, helpline or police. If you can't get hold of anyone directly in your life right now (maybe you are at home alone and it is like 2 a.m. — I get that, trust me!), then call a 24/7 helpline or the police.

You can do it!

This is probably the longest letter in this book, and that is because your life matters so very much.

All my love,

Jazz x

FEELING ACTIVELY SUICIDAL – TIPS AND TOOLS

BY DR KIRSTEN DAVIS FROM THE PSYCHOLOGY GROUP

Suicidal thoughts are your brain trying to find a solution to the problem of the distress you are experiencing. These tips and tools are not about solving all the problems that led you to this place of distress — they are about surviving the crisis without making it worse. They are skills to get through this one moment, and the next.

The one thing in life we can guarantee is change, and that includes knowing that the intensity of your emotions *can* change. Like waves in the ocean, your emotions will come and go. Let's surf these waves together . . .

To regulate intense emotions and help you to ride out the urge to act on suicidal thoughts:

* If you know the particular situation or situations that prompt thoughts of suicide, actively avoid these in the short term, if you can. This may not always be possible, but do your best.
* Solve the current problem that may be leading to thoughts of suicide. Ask for help if it is difficult. For example, say to a

close friend or family member, 'I really need your help. This has happened and I don't know what to do about it. I am feeling really overwhelmed — can you help me figure out what to do?'

* Confront unhelpful thoughts or actions directly — for example, the belief that others are better off without you is simply not true.

* Block any actions that involve thinking about or planning suicide. The pathway towards building a life worth living involves shutting the door to suicide.

* Regulating and reducing the intensity of your emotions will give your brain's prefrontal cortex a chance to be able to think more clearly about the next steps you need to take to get through this challenging time and see there is hope. Practise the following skills to help you get through moments of high distress.

THE STOPP SKILL

* **S**top — freeze. Pause for a moment. Your emotions may lead you to act without thinking. Stay in control.

* **T**ake a step back — physically or mentally. Mindfully pause what you were about to say or do. Take a deep breath and let it go.

* **O**bserve — notice what is going on inside and outside of you. What is the situation? What are your thoughts/feelings? What are others doing? What sensations do you notice in your body?

* **P**erspective — pull back. What is the bigger picture here? How might you or others see the situation differently?

* **P**roceed mindfully — act with awareness. When making a decision to act, consider the situation and the thoughts and

feelings of yourself and others. Ask yourself mindfully what actions will make things better — or worse. Practise what works.

THE 'CHILL' SKILL

This technique uses cold temperatures to regulate intense emotion. When your face is submerged in ice-cold water it elicits a 'dive reflex' response, which activates your parasympathetic (relax response) nervous system, slows your heart rate and reduces the experience of intense emotion in that moment. It is helpful for riding the wave of urges to act impulsively, to help ground you and connect you to the present, to decrease distress and to open the door to being skilful.

There are a few ways you can do this:

1. Fill a bowl with cold water and add ice. Bend over, hold your breath, and put your face in the water (up to your temples) for between 30 and 60 seconds, or until you start to become uncomfortable. Remove your face, and then repeat if needed.

2. Have an ice-cold swim or shower, or splash cold water on your face.

3. Use a zip-lock bag of ice, a cold flannel, gel face-mask, bag of frozen peas or an ice pack. Wrap it over your eyes, upper cheeks and temples if possible. Standing or seated, bend forward and take a deep breath, holding it for as long as you can or, rather than holding your breath, take ten slow, deep, belly-breaths. If it feels hard to catch your breath, just keep trying — every breath could be a little deeper. Drop and relax your shoulders.

If you feel cold and shaky afterwards, warm up — have a hot shower, get a wheat bag, wrap up in a warm blanket with a hot chocolate.

Note: If you have a heart condition, allergy, anorexia or bulimia, check with your doctor before trying this. Also, the effects are only short-lived, so it is important to repeat the practice again if necessary, and then practise another skill.

INTENSE EXERCISE
A fast burst of exercise can create an intense sensation, which reduces anxiety, quickly shifts your mood and helps you ride out urges. What can you do? Star jumps, a fast run around the block, press-ups, an intense gym workout. If your suicidal urges are high and going out will potentially increase your risk, choose an exercise activity you can do at home.

PACED BREATHING
Scientific evidence has shown that you can activate your parasympathetic nervous system through paced breathing — more specifically, by extending the length of your out breath.

Introducing a daily practice of breathing exercises is highly beneficial for reducing feelings of distress. It will help with training your relaxation response, so your body can more quickly relax when you most need it to.

Slow your breath to five or six breaths per minute (i.e. one complete breath cycle lasting ten to twelve seconds). For one minute, count the seconds you inhale and seconds you exhale. Choose a pattern in and out (maybe five seconds in, seven seconds out; or three in, five out).

For the next five minutes, practise this paced breathing. Remember, if your mind wanders, just bring it back to the breath.

THE
WORLD
NEEDS
YOU
HERE.

To read when you are feeling impulsive

Hello!

Breathe. Take a moment. This will pass.

These feelings and deep emotions you are experiencing right now — they will pass. Before you read what I've written to you, I want you to try some practical techniques right now to help calm yourself down, then let's come back and chat. Turn back to pages 88–92 and use the tools there to control your emotions.

Feeling a little bit calmer? If not, keep doing the things listed on pages 88–92 until you are, and then let's talk.

Your intrusive thoughts and emotions right now are valid, but they are just emotions. They are not facts.

I remember one time when I was in therapy, when my movie was just about to come out into the world and I was so overwhelmed and scared, and I said, 'This is going to be too much pressure and it's going to take me out.'

As soon as I said that, my therapist told me to stand up. At first I was hesitant, as I was like 'I am in a very emotional moment right now', but I trusted her. So I stood up. She then stood up as well and she walked over to me and stood very, very close to me. I remember feeling so uncomfortable and I began to stumble back, trying to get her out of my space. She said, 'Jazz, say that again.' I looked at her, confused, but eventually I said again, 'This is going to be too much pressure and it's going to take me out.'

She replied, 'Now I want you to say that same thing, but this time say "I am having the <u>thought</u> that this is going to be too much pressure and it's going to take me out".' I was so confused, but she kept prompting me to say it. I could feel my anxiety level hiking up — she was still so close to me — and so I said what she asked and she moved back a step. She kept doing this, and each time I would say the sentence she would walk a little further away.

She then explained that simply adding the words 'I am having the thought . . .' in front of any emotional statement, takes the statement one step away from you. It helps you to understand that it is simply a thought or an emotion, and that doesn't mean that it is a fact. It is important to acknowledge the thoughts and feelings, but in moments of panic and impulsivity, it is equally as important to take a step back and know that there is something that you can change.

Impulsivity can be scary — you feel so out of control. It is something that I have battled with for so much of my life and have really had to work hard on learning to manage. What

I can tell you is that it is possible to have these thoughts and impulses <u>and not act on them</u>. You can learn to sit in the wave of emotion, knowing that eventually it will pass.

My impulsivity as a teenager fuelled a lot of my self-harm and suicide attempts. I could be sitting on the thought for a while but would then suddenly have the urge to just run and act on it.

I remember so clearly after my last ever suicide attempt that I made a goal for myself that I would learn to sit through the impulses. One of the first things that I did was write a letter called 'Dear Suicidal Me'. I have talked about this letter a lot, but in case you haven't heard or read it, it is basically a letter that I wrote to myself <u>specifically for the moments that I was feeling impulsive and wanting to hurt myself</u>. I found that it is really hard to regulate yourself or have any form of clarity while you are in the middle of a wave of impulsive thoughts, and so I wrote this letter in advance. I filled it with people to contact, reasons to fight and things to do, and reminded myself of the well-known process if I gave into the impulse. This is what I wrote:

DEAR SUICIDAL ME,

IF YOU ARE READING THIS, THEN I AM GUESSING THAT THINGS AREN'T
GOING TOO WELL FOR YOU. I KNOW THAT IT PROBABLY SEEMS IMPOSSIBLE,
THAT YOU HAVE GONE AROUND IN ANOTHER CIRCLE AND THAT IT WOULD
BE BETTER WITH YOU GONE. YOU THINK YOU ARE A BURDEN TO EVERYONE
AROUND YOU AND THAT NO ONE COULD POSSIBLY LOVE YOU — BUT YOU
ARE WRONG. THERE ARE PEOPLE WHO LOVE YOU — YOU KNOW WHAT
YOU NEED TO DO TO BRING YOURSELF BACK UP FROM THIS SPACE. PUT
ON INSPIRATIONAL MUSIC (NOT SAD MUSIC LIKE YOU ALWAYS DO, YOU
KNOW THIS MAKES YOU FEEL WORSE, YET YOU STILL CHOOSE TO DO IT).
TEXT ESTHER, LIBBY OR WAYNE — REMEMBER, YOU ARE NOT ALONE AND
PEOPLE CARE, SO PLEASE GET OVER YOUR PRIDE AND FEAR AND REACH OUT
... THEY WOULD RATHER HAVE YOU MESSY AND ALIVE THAN NOT HERE AT
ALL. YOU KNOW THE PROCESS IF YOU TRY THIS AGAIN. HOSPITALS, POLICE
— YOU HAVE BEEN HERE BEFORE AND RIGHT NOW IN THIS MOMENT YOU
HAVE THE CHANCE FOR THAT TO NOT BE YOUR REALITY. YOU ARE SO CLOSE
TO BEING FREE OF ALL THIS, DON'T GIVE UP NOW ... REMEMBER WHO AND
WHAT YOU ARE FIGHTING FOR, PEOPLE DO CARE ABOUT YOU AND YOU HAVE
A FUTURE ... IT'S NOT ABOUT BATTLING YOUR PAST BUT FIGHTING FOR YOUR
FUTURE — START FIGHTING RIGHT NOW, TAKE THOSE STEPS ...

    YOU GOT THIS

    JAZZ

I encourage you to write a letter like this, for those moments when you are feeling impulsive and likely to act on your feelings. Key things to include are:

- ♥ who you are fighting for (family, friends, etc.)
- ♥ how to fight (who to call, listening to happy music, self-soothing tools, etc.)
- ♥ why you are fighting. Are you fighting for your family? For your future career? For your own future family?

This letter for me was an absolute lifesaver. I would pull it out when I was feeling these strong impulses and I would remind myself of the things I needed to do. I also had journal pages with details of who to call and practical tools that I could use in that moment to calm me down or distract my thinking.

There is so much power in your decisions. Right now, in this moment, you have the ability to not give in to your impulse. You have the ability to call someone, watch a TV show, shower . . . do anything else, and begin to change your own narrative.

It is hard, I know. It is decision after decision after decision, but it is so, so worth it. Because _you_ are worth it. You are worth fighting for and you are worth being here.

You deserve love and support, and you deserve to be happy. This moment will pass — it will not last forever. You've got this!

Breathe, read the tips and maybe write down some things that you can do for the next time you are feeling like this.

All my love,

Jazz

THERE IS SO MUCH POWER IN YOUR DECISIONS.

To read when you are having trouble with food

Hey friend,

Ah man, I am so sorry that you are struggling with this at the moment. While it is something that I personally have not dealt with, I know that this is an incredibly difficult and often all-consuming battle for so many people.

I want to introduce you to a friend of mine, Genevieve Mora. She co-founded Voices of Hope with me, and she battled with an eating disorder for a lot of her teenage years. I wanted her to write to you as someone who has been where you are and who has come through the other side, in the hope that she might encourage you to fight today.

And remember, you are not alone — ever.

Keep fighting.

All my love,

Jazz

HEY YOU,

I WANT TO START BY SAYING I SEE YOU AND I HEAR YOU. I AM RIGHT HERE, CHEERING YOU ON.

AS JAZZ SAID, THIS IS A BATTLE I KNOW ALL TOO WELL. ALTHOUGH OUR EXPERIENCES WON'T BE EXACTLY THE SAME, I WANT YOU TO KNOW THAT YOU ARE NOT ALONE IN YOUR FIGHT.

AS A TEENAGER, I WAS REALLY UNWELL WITH AN EATING DISORDER AND, DUE TO THIS, MY RELATIONSHIP WITH FOOD CONSUMED A LOT OF MY TIME. I WAS LUCKY ENOUGH TO LEARN MANY THINGS THROUGHOUT MY JOURNEY, BUT THE MOST IMPORTANT THING I LEARNT WAS THAT I AM WORTHY AND DESERVING OF FOOD. AND SO ARE YOU!

I KNOW THAT THERE ARE MANY REASONS PEOPLE STRUGGLE WITH FOOD, AND REGARDLESS OF WHAT THAT REASON IS FOR YOU, I HOPE THIS LETTER HELPS YOU REALISE THAT YOU CAN DO THIS.

FOOD IS ONE OF LIFE'S MOST BASIC NEEDS. YOU NEED FOOD TO SURVIVE, YOU NEED FOOD TO LIVE AND YOU ARE SO WORTHY OF A GREAT LIFE — PLEASE NEVER QUESTION THAT. PUSH THOSE NEGATIVE THOUGHTS TO THE SIDE AND REPEAT THESE MANTRAS OUT LOUD. I KNOW THIS MAY SOUND SILLY BUT POSITIVE SELF-TALK IS PROVEN TO CREATE CHANGE, AND WAS SOMETHING I USED A LOT THROUGHOUT MY OWN JOURNEY.

* I AM WORTHY OF FOOD.
* I DESERVE TO LIVE A FULL LIFE.
* I NEED TO NOURISH MYSELF IN ORDER TO THRIVE.
* FOOD IS NOT THE ENEMY.
* I CAN DO THIS.

WHEN I WAS STRUGGLING WITH MY RELATIONSHIP WITH FOOD, I FOUND
FOCUSING ON THE POSITIVES TO BE REALLY IMPORTANT — FOCUSING ON
THE THINGS THAT NOURISHING MYSELF PROPERLY WOULD ALLOW ME TO DO.

* IF I EAT I WILL HAVE MORE ENERGY.
* I WILL BE ABLE TO THINK MORE CLEARLY.
* I AM FACING MY FEARS HEAD-ON AND CHALLENGING ANY UNTRUE
  BELIEFS I HOLD.
* I WILL BE ABLE TO SOCIALISE MORE EASILY.
* I AM GETTING CLOSER TO A LIFE OF FREEDOM THAT I TRULY DESERVE.

IN THE MOMENTS WHEN I WAS STRUGGLING, I WOULD TRY AND THINK
ABOUT THE <u>WHY</u> — WHY IT IS IMPORTANT THAT I NOURISH MY BODY AND
SOUL, BECAUSE, LET ME TELL YOU, IT IS <u>SO</u> IMPORTANT. OUR BODIES ARE
INCREDIBLE THINGS. THEY PROTECT US, THEY SUPPORT US, THEY ALLOW US TO
EXPERIENCE ALL THAT WE DO, AND IN RETURN IT'S SO IMPORTANT WE GIVE
THEM THE LOVE AND CARE THEY NEED.

SO, TO YOU WHO ARE READING THIS, STRUGGLING WITH YOUR
RELATIONSHIP WITH FOOD, I CHALLENGE YOU TO DO SOMETHING ABOUT
IT. GO AND TELL A FRIEND OR A FAMILY MEMBER; GO AND GRAB A
SNACK; CREATE A VISION BOARD OR AN INSPIRING PLACEMAT; TALK TO A
PROFESSIONAL; AND KNOW THAT FOOD WILL NEVER HURT YOU AS MUCH AS
YOUR NEGATIVE THOUGHTS TOWARDS IT WILL.

THE BEST TIME TO START THIS HEALING JOURNEY IS RIGHT NOW.
I AM SENDING YOU LOTS OF LOVE AND POSITIVE THOUGHTS.
YOU'VE GOT THIS,
GEN XX

THE BEST
TIME TO
START THIS
HEALING
JOURNEY
IS RIGHT
NOW.

To read when you have the urge to self-harm

Hey you!

I am so sorry that you are feeling these urges right now, but I am so proud of you for turning to this page in the book. I know that would not have been easy.

Let me start by saying that your feelings and emotions are valid. I know when it comes to self-harm that a lot of people don't understand, and therefore can say things that can feel invalidating, minimising or dismissive. The reasons why people self-harm are always different depending on the individual, but I want you to know that you are not alone in this. These urges can be really strong and at times feel overpowering, but you are stronger.

There are a few practical things that I personally found really helpful when trying to fight off these urges:

1. If you can, take an ice-cold swim! Or a cold or hot shower.

2. Snuggle with a warm wheat bag or under a weighted blanket.

3. Ice cubes. I personally found this one really helpful! Get ice cubes from the freezer and grip them in your hand.
4. Grab some coloured markers and draw on your body. This one might not feel like it helps initially, but for some people the simple distraction of drawing on their skin can actually help ease their mind.
5. Submerge your face in cold water. I learnt in therapy a while ago that a sudden drastic temperature change can shock your system and calm you down, while pulling your focus onto your now-cold face. I have used this technique (it also helps with panic attacks) and I highly recommend trying it.

I know that right now this emotion probably feels really overwhelming for you — but know that this absolute peak emotional urge won't last forever. The urge will subside, you just have to wait it out. While giving into the urge will also make it subside, it will only be momentary, and then you are left being physically hurt. Instead, use the distraction techniques and wait out the urge, knowing that the peak of emotion will come back down. You won't feel like this forever.

You are so worth fighting for. Every minute that you choose to fight is a minute worth celebrating.

I encourage you to download the app 'I am sober' from the app store — it can help you track how long you have been self-harm-free, and sends you an alert on milestones like one week, ten days, one month, one year — it goes on!

So now I ask you, put down the blades or self-harm tools that you have. Throw them out if you can. Having them in your sight makes it harder for you to fight this urge. I know that it feels like a sense of security having them there, but I promise you it is quite the opposite. The best thing you can do right now is to throw them away. Take away the means of self-harm and know that this is a battle you are not fighting alone.

You are worth it. You can do it.

I believe in you.

All my love,

Jazz

SELF-HARM – TIPS AND TOOLS

BY DR KIRSTEN DAVIS FROM THE PSYCHOLOGY GROUP

1. Focus mindfully to create a pause in your thoughts and actions, buying time to recognise that you have a *choice* to act or not, rather than feeling unable to stop yourself acting on an urge.

2. Notice the urge you are feeling, but 'surf' it rather than act on it. An urge is what you feel just before you self-harm — it could be physical sensations (racing heart, feeling numb, disconnection from yourself), emotions or thoughts. No matter how intense it feels, surf the urge without giving in to it for as long as you can.

3. Remove access to what you may use to harm yourself.

4. Practise skills that get you through the moment and reduce intense emotional sensations, such as the STOPP or Chill skills, and paced breathing (see pages 89–92).

5. Distract yourself. Remember, it is about getting through a moment without making things worse. Move your mind away from what is causing the distress. Pay close attention to what is around you.

6. If possible, solve the problem that is causing the distress.

To read when you have relapsed

Hey you!

Listen to me: relapse is part of the journey. Relapse is part of recovery. It does not make you weak, it does not make you worth any less — it's OK. Don't beat yourself up over this.

I know that relapse can make you feel all kinds of things — anger at yourself for giving in, sadness, guilt, shame . . . all of the things that can then hold our minds captive and keep us dwelling on the mistake. Most people who are in recovery have relapsed — most more than once. I know that I did! Many times, in fact.

It doesn't matter how many times you fall; what matters is that you get back up afterwards. That you brush yourself off, admit the mistake, take note of what triggered it, adjust, and then start again. You can spend days beating yourself up over this, or you can put that energy into getting back on your feet and trying again. You made a mistake, you are <u>not</u> the mistake. Don't let this tell you otherwise.

What I have learnt in my own journey, and also from the people that I now walk life with, is that when it comes to relapse, shame is one of the most powerful emotions. Shame keeps you quiet, tells you that you are the problem and that you don't deserve help. One of the bravest things that you can do right now is to let someone in and tell them that you have relapsed. It doesn't have to be a big thing, but sharing with someone even that basic fact can help lift the isolating shame that can cause your mind to spiral. Be selective about who you tell — make sure it is someone who can help hold you accountable, but also just love you through the journey. You don't have to do this alone.

The other really important thing about telling someone that you have relapsed is that it can stop the thought pattern of 'Well, I broke it — now what is the point in going on fighting?', which we can use to justify relapsing time and time again.

I don't know what it is that you are fighting — people get addicted to all kinds of things: self-harm, drugs, alcohol, eating behaviours, porn . . . the list goes on and on. No matter what you are dealing with, there is hope for you. These addictions are not your identity. There are <u>so</u> many stories of people who have fought through these battles and won; people who fought through relapses, beliefs, behaviours and responses and who are in strong recovery. Just have a look online and I know you will find many inspiring stories.

The biggest reason that they got to where they are today is that they chose to get back up when they fell. Time and time again, they chose to get back up. And so to you I say: get back up, my friend.

Send the message, stay accountable.

You can do this. The journey starts again . . .

So much love,

Jazz

ADDICTION
IS NOT YOUR
IDENTITY.

To read when you are struggling with trauma

Hey there,

I am so sorry that you are struggling with trauma at the moment. Trauma comes in so many different ways and from so many different life experiences, from abuse, to bullying, loss, accidents, natural disasters . . . The dictionary describes trauma as: 'a deeply distressing or disturbing experience'.

Whatever that trauma is that you have experienced, I am so sorry. I am so sorry for your pain and how this has altered your life. What sucks so much about trauma is that it is not just the event itself that you have to deal with, but the mental and emotional aftermath. People respond and deal with trauma in so many ways. I am not a professional, but I can share with you my own experience.

Funnily enough, the timing of writing this letter is a little ironic — because I myself have just started trauma therapy. So, friend, I am right in this with you! I understand the pain of flashbacks, responses, fear, guilt, anger, sadness . . . I get it. I know how hard it is and how draining and overwhelming it can feel.

However, I am also beginning to see that the trauma we have experienced doesn't have to rule our lives forever — that while we can never change the experience, as much as we might want to, we can learn to change the way we respond, and we can see it slowly lose its emotional and mental grip on us.

I know that it can be so difficult to face — I think that is why it took me so long to finally agree to even doing trauma therapy (and by the way, it is _never_ too late to try trauma therapy!). While I had worked through so many of my life experiences and mental struggles, I had almost actively avoided facing and exploring the deep reality of my key traumas, because I was afraid of what it might bring up. I was afraid that I wouldn't be able to handle it. I was scared of having to say them out loud and how much more real that would make them feel. I was worried about what my therapist would think, and that her perception of me might change and reinforce beliefs I already had about myself (I will expand on this soon). But let me tell you, I know that for me personally, having trauma therapy is one of the best decisions I have made. There are times (many) where I hate it, but a couple of months in and I can already see the difference in how I think and feel.

I am someone who shares my past struggles with the world, but very seldom do I share my current journey. I think that is because I like to be able to share it alongside hope and with clarity, having worked to overcome it. However, in this letter I want to share with you my current experiences of trauma counselling, in the hope that it will help you feel a little less alone and maybe even encourage you to get help.

A really important part of it is learning tools and things that you can do to help you in the moments where the trauma feels overwhelming. For example, one day my therapist and I were talking about emotional regulation. As we were talking, a memory that I didn't even realise I had was triggered. I began having flashbacks and suddenly felt overwhelmed.

My therapist noticed this, and began to softly tell me to reposition myself and to put my feet on the floor. She encouraged me to bend down and get my water bottle, and adjust my physical position. I didn't realise it at the time, but now I know that simply repositioning yourself can help to remind you that you are not back in the trauma, that you are physically safe and you are OK. She also showed me what happens when you put a cold-pack on your face, or put your face in cold water (see the tips on page 90). This is a really great way to regulate your emotions when you are feeling overwhelmed to the point of feeling paralysed. There are also a few more quick, practical tips that you can use when you are actively dealing with flashbacks and trauma-related responses on page 118.

At the start of each session, my therapist will ask me,

'What is the worst thing that could happen with you talking in detail about this trauma today?' My answers to this have varied as we have gone along, but one that I would like to share with you is an overwhelming fear that if I speak about it, I won't be able to pull myself back out of the emotion and flashbacks of it. This is a very legitimate and justified fear. However, each time this fear comes up, she will remind me that every time that I have dealt with flashbacks and felt like I could never get out of that emotion, I had always made it out. I'm not saying it was easy in any way, but it does mean that the flashbacks did not rule my life, and that in fact I was stronger than these memories, even when it didn't feel like I was.

Trauma in my life has led me to feel and believe all kinds of things. I have felt like I was 'too broken' and that I was a terrible person; I have felt guilty that I didn't do enough; I have experienced anger and overwhelming shame. Yet what I have found is that the more that I talk to someone about my experiences, the less grip these things have on me, and the more I begin to recognise that some of my beliefs, while understandable, are just not true. The trauma that I have experienced does not make me 'too broken' or make me a terrible person, but is something that I went through and survived in the best way that I could at that time.

While I may not know what you have gone through, what has happened in your life or how you are feeling at the moment, what I do know is that talking about it in a safe environment is one of the best ways to help challenge the negative beliefs that you have about the situation. It's like another lens that is able to see wider than our own lens, through which we could only see what was right in front of us at the time.

What I have learnt is that trauma does not have to define you. It is not a part of your identity, but is something that you lived through — and you are still here.

I don't know what you have experienced, but I do know that it is possible for you to work through it and get to a point where it doesn't rule your life, thinking and behaviours anymore. The first step? Ask for help. You don't have to do this by yourself. You don't have to carry this heavy weight alone. Even if you're not in the place to see a professional right now, let someone in your world that you trust know that you are struggling with it.

Learn as many tools as you can (there are lots online too!), and remember that you are so very worth fighting for.

You are not your trauma.

You are not alone.

All my love,

Jazz x

YOU SURVIVED
IN THE *best* WAY
THAT YOU *could*
AT THAT TIME.

STRUGGLING WITH TRAUMA AND FLASHBACKS – TIPS AND TOOLS

BY DR KIRSTEN DAVIS FROM THE PSYCHOLOGY GROUP

When trauma memories show up, our fight/flight nervous system activates. Our body reacts as though the traumatic event is happening right now. We need to connect to this present moment to let our brain know that we are not in the past. When our brain is scared, we have little flexibility — we can't think freely. The primitive part of your brain (the amygdala) gets emotionally hijacked and revs up — that is why you feel so overwhelmed with emotion and uncomfortable physical sensations.

Sometimes our alarm systems are sloppy and there is a loose connection somewhere, so they get tripped off when there is no actual threat. The goal over time is to gradually transform old brain circuits that are conditioned to act with fear.

Here are some things you can do to return yourself to the present moment:

1. Ground yourself: anchor your feet on the floor, place your hand on something close by, and feel the sensation of what it touches.

2. Observe your breath. Practise paced breathing (see page 91).
3. Practise mindfulness (see page 217). Take a mindful pause in which you step back and breathe, giving your brain's prefrontal cortex (the part which helps us take the information, consider options and produce an adaptive response) a chance to catch up. Observe and describe to yourself what is happening in that moment.
4. Use movement: the sensory experience of movement and balance alterations can settle you (like going for a brisk walk, stretching, yoga, swinging, bouncing on a trampoline).
5. Experiment with letting flashbacks come and go, like a train coming in and out of the station. Remind yourself 'this too shall pass'.
6. Be aware of your present safe environment.

To read when you feel like you are slipping into old habits

Hey friend,

So, you feel like you are slipping back into old habits again? I am really glad that you have chosen to turn to this letter in this moment, because it means that you recognise that you are starting to go back into them, but it also means that you want to fight against it.

Remember that recovery is a journey — a long road, with all kinds of turns and bumps and unexpected moments that can put you back in a position or mindset where you find yourself facing these old habits again. The very simple fact that for you this is referred to as an 'old habit' suggests that you already have fought to overcome this before. <u>You have already done it.</u> That means that you can do it again, and again, and again.

Don't beat yourself up over this. Instead, we notice it, ask for help, find the things that we can do to change, and then we go again. I say 'we' because although I am on the other side of my most intense mental health journey, there are still behaviours, habits and responses that I have to fight off as they try to re-enter my life — habits that I picked up as a result of a whole lot of different situations and circumstances, events and relationships in my life. Naturally, when life gets a little messy again, these things can pop back into my mind — behaviours like isolating from people rather than asking for help, or over-working to hide my emotions. So you are not alone in this — at all!

A few things that I have found helpful when I have noticed myself slipping back into old habits is to always tell someone the moment that I realise I'm doing it. Don't wait for it to become a habit once again — once you notice it, let someone in your world know. This helps create accountability and someone to check in with and encourage you. It doesn't mean that the person is going to think 'Oh my gosh, they are back to being the same person they used to be'. You can try to word it like 'I have just noticed recently that I am starting to do X again. I want to fight through this and make sure it doesn't become a habit again, and I just want to tell you so that you can keep me accountable on making progress to work through it.'

One of my habits from when I was a teenager was that when I was feeling really emotional or battling with something, I would withdraw from everyone and assume that I had to cope with it on my own. I would ignore people's messages and hide away. I knew this habit always led to me feeling even worse, believing that I was alone, and then my problems would escalate. This is still a response that I know I have to be super-active in not allowing back into my life. I will now make a habit of messaging someone close to me and letting them know if I am struggling. That simply gives them knowledge, and then permission to check in on me and see what I need, but more importantly, it means I know that I have people and don't need to isolate.

Whether it be self-harm, addictions, responses, destructive behaviours or anything in between, you don't have to do this alone. You are strong, you are brave and this does not have to consume your life. You are worth fighting for. You are worth picking up the phone and telling someone, worth booking in to see a counsellor, talking to a teacher, going back to the doctor. (If the idea of doing these things scares you, then turn to Part 4, which starts on page 161 and is all about asking for help!)

You are worth more than these old habits.

You have got this!

Fight, fight, fight!

All my love,

Jazz

To read when you are struggling to sleep

Hey you!

You are in good company with this letter. Sleep is something that I have struggled with for years, and something that I continue to struggle with now. Not being able to sleep is so difficult, especially as it is essential to function as a human!

Whether it is stress, worry, fear or even just an inability to stop your mind, not being able to sleep is dreadful. For me the reasons that I have struggled to sleep have varied through the years. For some time it was trauma and flashbacks that kept me awake, then stress, fear — and the biggest player, an overactive mind!

Dealing with an overactive mind at night is so frustrating. It is something that I have experienced for a long time and have often struggled to articulate to people. I wish that I could just record what my brain is like and then play the tape so others can understand! For years, people would say, 'Oh, is it because you're stressed?', and while at times stress definitely kept me up, that wasn't really what I was dealing with. The best way I can describe it is that it is like having about 30 different internet tabs open, and I am jumping from thought to thought, physically unable to quieten my mind. I would try to tell myself, 'OK, on the count of three I will just stop thinking . . .' and then about one and a half seconds later I would be onto something else!

I have come to learn that for me personally, it is actually my ADHD that causes my brain to be constantly overactive — but this is also something that I know many others struggle with, too. There are a few things that I have found to help with my overactive mind at night (all of which are also really good if stress is the thing keeping you awake).

One is putting my phone down at least an hour before I go to bed. We often hear that you shouldn't have screen-time before bed, but I know many of us (including me) are guilty of holding our phones right until we decide to go to sleep. The scrolling, blue light and shots of dopamine are not helping your mind calm down before bed — it needs to unwind once you finally put the phone down and try to sleep.

Another thing I find helpful is to write out in detail my plan for the next day: what time I have to be awake, what I have to do and where I have to be, and everything in between. This stops my mind from wandering into details and gives me one less thing to think about.

I also started sleeping with a pen and paper next to my bed, so that when I have a thought as I am trying to drift off to sleep that I just can't get rid of or am spending time thinking about (usually ideas or things I need to do), instead of lying there trying to stop thinking about it or worrying I will forget it, I grab the paper and write it down. That gets it out of my head, and I know that I will remember it the next day and can deal with it then.

A final suggestion for an overactive mind is using meditation, or listening to podcasts. I personally found that sleep podcasts (I listen to Sleep with Me) are really helpful, because they make my mind focus on just the one thing I am listening to. The host is strategically boring but also interesting enough to listen to, and their voice drifts off as I drift off to sleep.

I know there will be people reading this letter who may be struggling to sleep because of trauma — I understand this pain, too. The flashbacks, fear and feeling out of control can be paralysing. I want you to know that you are not alone in this, and that right now in this moment you are safe. It is really important that you talk to someone if you haven't already and get some proper professional help (read some more about this on page 184).

For now though, in this moment, you can try to use the grounding technique that I talked about in the letter to read when you are anxious — it is a really good tool to help remind you that right now, in this moment, you are safe, and that you are not in the situation you were in when you were getting hurt. The method is to notice:

five things that you can see

four things that you can touch

three things that you can hear

two things you can smell

one thing you can taste.

Here are some more tips that can help if you are struggling with flashbacks at night (or just have trouble getting to sleep):

♥ Keep to a sleep schedule. As much as you can, try to go to bed and wake up at the same time every day. This helps your mind and body feel more prepared when it is time to sleep.

♥ Do something relaxing before bed. Meditation, showering, reading — anything that can help your mind and body be at ease before you go to bed.

♥ Sleep in places where you feel safe. If your environment or bedroom doesn't make you feel safe, then see what you can do to change that. Maybe you could buy a new duvet cover, change your pillows or keep a dim light on.

I am so sorry for whatever has happened to you that is causing you the flashbacks, panic or insomnia. No one deserves to suffer through that pain. Yet despite what you went through, you did the most important and bravest thing possible and you survived. <u>You survived.</u>

Whatever is keeping you awake right now, try to engage

in some of the tools mentioned here, and know that you are not alone. It is OK to ask for help, and there are so many resources available for you to try — just look online (but not right before bed)!

One last thing: don't try to force sleep. Professionals say that if you can't fall asleep in 20 minutes, then get out of bed and do something relaxing until you feel tired, then try again. I know that sounds exhausting, but it really helps your body to associate being in bed with winding down and going to sleep.

You've got this.

All my love,

Jazz

YOU ARE WORTHY. YOU ARE LOVED. YOU ARE WANTED.

PART 3:

Beliefs

To read when you feel like a burden

Hey you!

First of all, let me tell you that I understand this feeling like no other. I know what it is to feel afraid to speak up out of fear of being a burden to other people. I know the feeling of believing that you are 'too much' for people to handle. This feeling and belief can be so debilitating to experience, but I want to assure you right now, as someone on the other side, that you are <u>not</u> a burden.

You are hurting, and you are deserving of support, no matter how many times you have been in this position before. I see you. I hear you. I understand.

The pain of this feeling and belief can feel so incredibly heavy. It actually has a lot more mental impact than many people might think. You've got the reality of battling with mental illness and everything that comes with it, and then you add the weight of feeling like your pain and your struggles are burdening everyone else around you.

I actually think this was one of the most difficult things

in my journey. I would spend hours and hours of my time thinking about how much I was putting other people through, and how their lives would be easier without me in them. For a long time I was so afraid to speak up when I was struggling because I felt like I was going in continuous circles that were hurting people around me — circles that would see them have to talk me through a crisis, take me to hospital again, or see me break down one more time.

There were many people who came in and out of my life during this time. There were people who told me that I was too much to handle (out of a lack of understanding). There were people who felt like they had to 'fix' me, and when they were unable to, they walked away. This eventually built the belief in me that I was 'too much', and I began to fear reaching out because I assumed that people didn't want to hear about what I was experiencing, or that I was burdening them.

If you have read my first book, 'Stop Surviving, Start Fighting', then you will know of a special woman in my life, Esther. I've shared frequently about the conversation that I had with Esther around surviving versus fighting and how that concept changed my life, but what a lot of people didn't see were the years of life we had walked together beforehand.

I first met Esther when I was 12 years old and very, very broken. After a few years I ended up at the same church as her, and she became someone in my life who began to walk with me through my struggles. Esther was often the person who would receive my goodbye messages, or calls telling her I was in hospital. There were times that I would physically run away, when I would create drama, and many, many moments when I would just cry uncontrollably. She saw the worst of my responses and behaviour, the defence mechanisms I had built and the webs I spun trying to protect myself.

I found myself trying to solve a lot of my issues alone because I didn't want to burden her, and wouldn't reach out until I eventually realised that I couldn't do it alone and things imploded. That pattern led to heart-wrenching feelings of being a burden, then spiralling into thinking that other people's lives would be easier without me.

However, I have now come to understand that over the years that my brain kept telling me that I was burdening Esther, she didn't ever see it that way. That's not to say that it wasn't difficult for her to deal with, because my goodness, I know that it would have been — but she never saw me in the way I saw myself.

I have asked Esther to write a letter here, to show you that those who love you really do care, and they want you to know hope and find joy. It is my hope that her letter helps you see that even though you feel like a burden, you are not. And so to you, here is a letter to encourage you to keep going — from the person who knows what it is to be the helping hand.

DEAR YOU,
LET ME TELL YOU, YOU ARE NOT A BURDEN. LET'S START BY DEFINING WHAT
A BURDEN IS.

> BURDEN: SOMETHING WHICH IS BORNE WITH DIFFICULTY; AN
> OBLIGATION.

NOW LET'S LOOK AT ANOTHER CONCEPT, TO BELONG.

> TO BELONG: TO BE IN A PROPER SITUATION; TO BE PART OF A GROUP;
> TO BE ATTACHED OR BOUND BY BIRTH OR ALLEGIANCE.

THERE IS A GREAT DIFFERENCE BETWEEN THOSE TWO CONCEPTS. THEIR
EXPRESSION OR BEHAVIOURS MIGHT LOOK THE SAME, BUT THEY ARE
ROOTED IN TWO DIFFERENT SOURCES AND THEREFORE HAVE TWO DIFFERENT
RESULTS. ONE IS ROOTED IN OBLIGATION — A 'HAVE TO'; ACTIONS TAKEN
WITH GREAT DIFFICULTY THAT ARE MOST LIKELY FORCED; ITS RESULTS ARE
SHORT-LIVED, INTERIM SOLUTIONS. THE OTHER COMES FROM A PLACE OF
INTERCONNECTED WILLINGNESS, WHERE ACTIONS ARE TAKEN WITH CARE
AND INTENTION, AND FROM LOVE. ITS RESULTS ARE SMALL, INCREMENTAL
WINS THAT ARE USUALLY LONG-LASTING.
YOU SEE THE TIME SPENT, THE MEALS, COFFEES, ENCOURAGING WORDS,
HARD CONVERSATIONS, TEXT RESPONSES AND THINK, WHY? WHY WOULD
ANYONE DO THIS, WHEN I HAVE NOTHING TO OFFER THEM? WHEN THEY

HAVE THEIR OWN FAMILIES, THEIR OWN LIVES TO ATTEND TO, WHY ARE THEY ATTENDING TO MINE? BUT THAT'S YOU SEEING ONLY FROM YOUR PERSPECTIVE. YOU SEE THE WORK OF A WEIGHTY BURDEN. I SEE THE WORK OF WORTHY BELONGING. IT IS THE DIFFERENCE BETWEEN SPENDING IN WASTE AND SPENDING TO INVEST. YOU ARE NOT A BURDEN, BECAUSE YOU BELONG.

THE WORK OF BELONGING TAKES TIME. IT HAS TO GENTLY BUT PERSISTENTLY ASSIST YOU IN UNLEARNING THOUGHT PATTERNS OF REJECTION, LONELINESS AND UNWORTHINESS. THE WORK OF BELONGING ISN'T ABOUT GRAND GESTURES OR SOMEONE DOING THE WORK FOR YOU — IT IS ABOUT THE ORDINARY EVERYDAY, WHERE YOU DO THE WORK AND I COMMIT TO WALK ALONGSIDE YOU. IN THIS WAY, PEOPLE WANT TO INVEST ENCOURAGEMENT, TIME AND RESOURCES IN YOU BECAUSE THEY KNOW IT CAN BUILD RESILIENCE AND NOT CO-DEPENDENCE.

AND SLOWLY BUT SURELY, WITH CONSISTENCY, YOU WILL LEARN THAT THIS IS NOT THE WORK OF CARRYING A HEAVY BURDEN. YOU <u>BELONG</u>. PEOPLE ARE THERE FOR YOU — NOT JUST IN THE BAD TIMES, BUT IN THE GOOD AND, MORE IMPORTANTLY, IN THE MUNDANE. IN THE EVERYDAY, ORDINARY LIVING OF LIFE, YOU WILL LEARN THAT YOU HAVE A PLACE, THAT YOU BELONG. THAT'S WHY YOU CAN'T GIVE UP. YOU ARE NOT A BURDEN, BECAUSE YOU BELONG.

ESTHER X

<u>You are not a burden, because you belong.</u> To you, the person who is reading this right now: <u>you belong</u>.

You may <u>have</u> a burden, but you <u>are not</u> a burden.

Reach out for help. Those you are afraid of burdening would much rather have you messy and alive than not here at all.

You've got this.

All my love,

Jazz

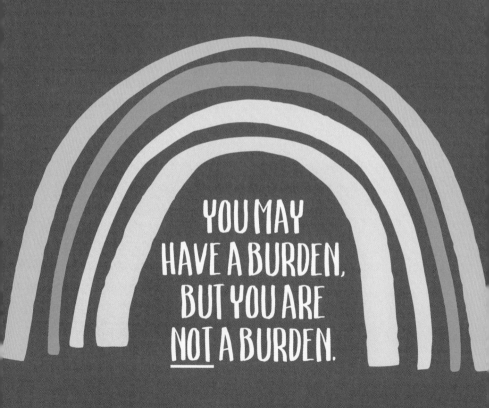

YOU MAY
HAVE A BURDEN,
BUT YOU ARE
NOT A BURDEN.

To read when you don't feel like you are enough

♡

Hey friend,

All right, let me start this by saying that you are _more_ than enough. You, just as you are — _you_ are enough.

I don't know if you have been told that you aren't enough, or if you are comparing yourself with others, but what I do know is that I think all of us feel at times like we are not enough. It was something that I felt for a lot of my life, and to be honest is something that I still battle with now!

Someone very close to me has always been really intentional about saying to me, 'Jazz, I love you for who you are — not what you do.' I think that often it can be really easy to get caught up in placing our worth and identity in the things we do or say — the way we act and our behaviours, meaning that our worth changes depending on these things. However, that is simply not true.

I know it can be so overwhelming battling the feeling that you will never measure up — that everyone else is better, or that they deserve things more than you. This was something that I personally felt for many years. I still sometimes find myself questioning why I ended up being the one able to write the book, share the story, direct the films, speak around the world. I start comparing myself with others, believing that they would be so much better at these things than I am, and get bogged down with 'I'm not good enough for this'.

I'm not saying this is healthy — I'm telling you this purely so that you can know that you are not alone. All of us question our worth and 'enoughness' from time to time, but what is important to understand is that <u>you are unique</u>. There are things that you bring to this world that are needed. Actions, ideas and perspectives that only you can bring. <u>You are needed</u>.

The process of realising that you are enough just for who you are and not what you do is a hard one. It is one that takes years and honestly, many of us are still on that journey with you. I spent so much of my life believing that I always had to be busy — I always had to be over-working to have any worth. I would push myself beyond measure, hoping that doing so would help fill this hole of feeling like I didn't belong.

I had been told for a lot of my life that I wasn't enough, that I didn't measure up. I wasn't ever the smartest in the class, the fastest on the field, I wasn't the best dancer or singer (in fact, I was definitely the worst singer, hah!). The only thing I seemed to come out on top of was constant drama — not something you want to be good at!

However, what I have come to learn is that my worth has nothing to do with the things that I can or can't do. It has nothing to do with things I have done in my past, my behaviours or my actions. It is not about the good things I have done, or my successes in life.

You are worth more than you will ever know. I know that at times life and people can make you feel less, or make you question your worth — and while I do not know what you have faced in your life, what obstacles you have battled through, what I do know is that as a human being, as you are right now, you are enough.

The very chances of you actually existing are so out of this world — and yet here you are. We have you. There is something that you have that the world was missing until you came. I don't mean to get soppy, but friend, you need to know that you, just as you are . . . you are enough.

I know that it can be so easy to compare yourself with others — especially in this world of social media — but I promise you that every single person you look at and think 'Wow, I wish I had their life', they too struggle and probably think the same thing about someone else at times. We must be so careful that we don't measure our worth against others' successes, stories, status or anything else. Your favourite sports player or actor or business leader — as a human being, you are worth just as much as they are. Why? Because the simple fact that we are all human means that our lives are of equal worth. I know it can be hard to see that, or believe that — trust me, it is something that I still struggle with, too.

I think that society has developed this belief that some lives are worth more than others. We can see this echoed in so many areas of our world — from race to wealth and status or power. However, at the end of the day, no matter what society portrays, we are all the same. We are all people and you, _you_ are enough.

You have to stop looking for external things to bring you worth and begin to invest in discovering how amazing you are. You don't have to be the most successful business person or top sports player — you don't have to have a large following on social media or be the best in your class. You just have to be _you_.

Again, please know that you are not alone in feeling this. This is something that we can journey together. We can do things like unfollow people on social media who make us feel like we are worth any less. (This is an OK thing to do, by the way — unfollowing someone doesn't mean that you don't like them, it just means that you are filtering the content that you see every day.) We can try saying affirmations out loud to ourselves in the morning, reminding ourselves that we are enough.

As this letter comes to an end, I want you to try something. Grab a pen and write down three things that you like about yourself. I know, sounds cheesy — but trust me, it's a good thing for you to put time into thinking about. Is it that you are a good friend? That you are funny? Loyal? Empathetic? Give it a go . . .

And remember, you are enough.

All my love,

Jazz

STOP LOOKING FOR EXTERNAL THINGS TO BRING YOU WORTH AND BEGIN TO INVEST IN DISCOVERING HOW AMAZING YOU ARE.

To read when you are feeling unlovable

Hey!

Oh man, I am so sorry that you are feeling this way. This is a feeling and belief that I know all too well, and I know how difficult and heart-breaking it can be. I know the pain of hearing people say 'I love you' and having the automatic internal response '<u>No you don't</u>'. One of the key, basic human needs is love, so when your brain is telling you that you are unlovable it can fuel many feelings and responses — all of them bad!

Let me tell you now that you are loved — and, just as importantly, that you are <u>not</u> unlovable. You are worthy of being loved, and I can guarantee that there are people in your world who love you. For many that is family; for others it may be friends or other people close to you. But there is a good chance that either your past experiences or own internal beliefs are blocking you from seeing it.

I really struggled with this belief for so many years. It was caused by a mixture of things that had happened to me and things people had said to me, but also I think a lot of it was fuelled by self-hatred — this idea that if I couldn't love myself, then why would anyone else? I assumed that everyone else viewed me the way that I viewed myself — that I was just a burden, a waste of space; that I was 'too much to handle.' and that people only cared because they felt they had to. At that time I had friends in my life and people who very much did love me, but I projected my own beliefs onto them. It was almost as if I was saying that they were lying when they said they loved me, because I knew there could be no possible way that was true.

But let me tell you this: most of the people who were telling me they loved me when I believed I was unlovable are the same people who are still in my world today. I now know without a doubt that these people love me for who I am. These people became my family and are my closest friends. Their love for me never changed — the difference is that now I have learnt that I am not unlovable. It has taken years of journeying but now I understand that I am worthy of being loved, even with my history and all of my mess. I, as a human being, am not unlovable.

And let me say this: people love you. They may not know how to show it properly, and maybe at times they make mistakes or talk and act in ways that are very human. But your brain will be filtering every response and word to try to fit your idea and belief that you are unlovable.

Let me give you an example: I remember one time when I was at a conference with someone who is a very close friend of mine and has been for many years. I saw her walking towards me in the hallway but as we got closer, she walked straight past me without saying hi. In that moment, my mind took that ten-second experience and told me, 'See, she thinks you are a burden. You're unlovable, Jazz.' It was as if I was taking a square and trying to fit it into a triangular hole! I was squashing and reshaping the experience to fit the mould of the belief in my mind that I was unlovable. However, I later came to realise that my friend was running late to a sound-check, and so was just focused on getting to the stage. It had nothing to do with her not loving me, nothing to do with me being a burden. In fact, that situation <u>had nothing to do with me at all!</u>

Let me say it again: you are not unlovable. No matter what you have done, or what has happened to you — you are not unlovable.

One thing that I did to help with this feeling was go through my messages and find any from those closest to me that said anything along the lines of that they loved me or they believed in me. I copied and pasted them into the Notes folder in my phone, and put the person's name next to their message. I used this collection of messages as 'evidence' to my brain that even though I thought I was unlovable, this is what the people closest to me were saying.

If you don't have many messages like that in your phone, then I encourage you to do a really brave thing: tell a couple of people you are closest to that you are struggling with this, and ask if they can write you a note or a message that you can hold onto for when you are feeling this way.

In addition to that, I also copied these messages into my journal. Alongside the messages, I wrote down practical things that those people had done <u>to show</u> that they loved me — things like still being there for me after five years, coming to see me in hospital, asking me to hang out with them, etc. A big one for me was to remember that a couple of these people knew all of my faults, had seen a lot of my journey and were still here with me — that in itself was evidence that if they could still love me despite knowing so much about me, then maybe the belief that I was unlovable because of these things <u>was not true</u>.

I don't know what has made you feel this way. Maybe you don't even know why you feel this way — but as someone who has been there, as someone who has felt this and believed it wholeheartedly, let me tell you, <u>it is not true</u>.

You are loved.
You are wanted.
You are important.
You matter.

Sending you so much love,
Jazz x

YOU ARE NOT UNLOVABLE.

To read when you feel like there is no hope

❀

Hi there!

If you have followed me or know my story, you may know that the number-one phrase that I say is 'Hope is real and change is possible'. I don't just say this as a cheesy quote — these are words and truths that I absolutely live by and believe.

I think that's because for a lot of my life I wholeheartedly believed the opposite. To me, hope was nothing but a meaningless four-letter word, and change was a concept applicable to everything other than my life. Weather could change, trends could change, seasons could change, friends could change — but my struggles could never change. I had pretty much accepted that this was the way my life would always be. That, however, was far from true.

Life can be really, really difficult, and when you are in the midst of hardship or difficult experiences it can be really hard to see a way out. All you are seeing every single day is the reality of your current circumstances. That can feel really overwhelming and make the concept of change seem impossible. You may be struggling with mental illness, poverty, feeling like you will never be enough, or so many other things. However, there are stories upon stories all around us that prove to us that no matter what it is that you are facing, hope is very real and change is possible.

Many of you would have heard the outline of my story — suffering childhood sexual abuse and battling mental illness. However, I am very aware that what you see in front of you today is the woman who advocates and stands on stages or makes TikTok videos, always smiling. I know it can be really difficult to understand or comprehend someone's struggles, or that they were once where you are, when all you see now is 'success'. So I want to give you a further glimpse into what was probably the lowest part of my story, to try to break down the barrier of why I felt for so many years that change would never be possible.

The particular time that I think illustrates this best was my last psych-ward admission. At this point, absolutely everything in my life had turned on its head. For starters, I had recently been fired from my job because of my mental health issues, so I was absolutely broke and going into major debt. I got kicked out of the place that I was living in, and I had no money to pay rent or even try to get myself into a new place. About eight months prior to this I had walked away from my entire community of people, including those who knew me the best, and had totally cut myself off. (For context, I left my actual family when I was 16, for my own mental health reasons.) I had spent the years since I moved out of home in and out of hospital, and was living in a self-destructive way, blowing apart any form of relationship as a way to protect myself from being hurt. I had isolated myself to the point where I literally didn't have an emergency contact to put on my hospital file. Not only was I jobless, broke, homeless and isolated, I was battling a nine-year struggle with mental illness and was now sitting in the intensive-care unit of a psychiatric ward.

I remember sitting in that ward and thinking to myself, 'This is it . . . there is no way out of this. This is just the way that my life will be.'

But I was _so_ wrong.

Not only would I learn how to fight back and eventually get discharged from mental health services, but I would see relationships restored, hope ignited and things that I had accepted as my normality begin to change. Nothing changed magically overnight, but as I persisted in the process and kept choosing to stay another day and engage in the fight, I did see change occur. In fact, change is still happening. I am still growing, learning and changing old responses. But I have learnt that no matter how dark a situation may be, <u>there is always hope</u>.

I wish so much that I could have understood this back when I was struggling, so I asked a favour of my friend Esther, who had such a huge impact on my life and my decision to fight. I asked her to write a letter to younger Jazz — the Jazz who may have been feeling or struggling with the same things that you are now.

DEAR YOUNGER JAZZ,

I SEE THE LOOK IN YOUR EYES WHEN I SAY PHRASES LIKE 'I'M HERE FOR YOU', AND 'YOU MAY NOT BELIEVE THIS NOW, BUT ONE DAY YOU WILL — YOU ARE WORTH IT'. YOUR EYES EXPOSE A MIXTURE OF CONFUSION, DISBELIEF, SUSPICION AND JUST A TINY BIT OF HOPE. AND I KNOW THAT THAT GLIMMER OF HOPE IS ALL YOU NEED, FOR NOW. THAT SMALL GLIMMER IS ALL YOU NEED TO 'STOP SURVIVING AND START FIGHTING'. AND THAT SMALL GLIMMER CHANGES EVERYTHING.

I'M NOT SURE IF YOU KNOW IT YET, IF YOU EVEN REALISE YOU HAVE HOPE IN YOU; BUT <u>I</u> KNOW IT, AND FOR NOW MY JOB IS CLEAR — IT'S TO HELP YOU TO <u>SEE</u> THAT HOPE THAT LIVES IN YOU. IT IS IN EVERY TEXT THAT ASKS IF I HAVE TIME FOR A 'CHAT'. IT IS IN EVERY TIME YOU SHOW UP FOR THAT CHAT. IT IS IN EVERY CONVERSATION WE HAVE WHERE YOU ARE OPEN AND HONEST ABOUT WHAT'S GOING ON WITH YOU. IT IS IN EVERY MOMENT WHERE YOU START TO BELIEVE THE ENCOURAGEMENT IN THAT CONVERSATION. IT IS IN EVERY THERAPY SESSION THAT YOU ATTEND (WHETHER IT WENT WELL OR NOT). IT IS IN EVERY TIME YOU TURNED UP TO WORK, CHURCH, GYM OR STUDY. IT IS IN EVERY BREATH THAT YOU STILL BREATHE. IT IS IN EVERY TEAR CRIED BECAUSE WORDS FAILED YOU. IT IS IN

EVERY HUG WE EXCHANGED, AND EVERY COFFEE CONSUMED, TOO (THERE ARE LOTS OF THOSE)! IT IS IN EVERY DEEP BREATH, JOINED WITH THE DECISION TO TRY AGAIN. IT IS IN EVERY ONE OF THOSE DARK DAYS, WHEN YOU DID NOTHING ELSE BUT DECIDE TO KEEP LIVING. IT IS IN THAT MOMENT WHERE YOU START BELIEVING THE WORDS OF THOSE AROUND YOU — THAT YOU ARE WANTED, TREASURED, LOVED; YOU HAVE A PLACE TO BELONG.

AND JUST LIKE THAT — NOT AFTER ONE DAY, BUT MANY DAYS; NOT ONE MONTH, BUT MANY MONTHS — THAT GLIMMER OF HOPE TURNS INTO A FLAME. IT STARTS TO CHASE AWAY THE DARK DAYS AND THE THOUGHTS THAT COME WITH THEM. AND IT BURNS BRIGHT ENOUGH THAT YOU CAN NO LONGER DENY: THERE IS HOPE.

THERE IS HOPE THAT ONE DAY, YOU WILL HAVE MORE GOOD DAYS THAN BAD. HOPE THAT YOUR ENERGY WILL NOT BE CONSUMED BY JUST BREATHING, BUT SPENT ON LIVING. HOPE THAT YOU WOULD LIVE IN A COMMUNITY, A FAMILY WHERE YOU ARE LOVED AND ACCEPTED.

BUT THE THING WITH HOPE IS THAT IT FLOATS. IT'S BUOYANT, ABLE TO STAY ABOVE THE WATER, EVEN IN A STORM. AND EVEN ON YOUR DARKEST DAYS, I COULD SEE THAT HOPE IN YOU.

YOU WEREN'T A BURDEN, BECAUSE THERE WAS A TINY GLIMMER OF HOPE. THAT TINY GLIMMER WAS SMALL ENOUGH TO MISS, BUT BIG ENOUGH TO CHANGE EVERYTHING. YOU WEREN'T A BURDEN, BECAUSE ALL I NEEDED TO DO WAS HOLD UP A MIRROR SO YOU COULD SEE THAT HOPE, TOO. BECAUSE OF THAT HOPE, I COULD ANSWER ANOTHER TEXT MESSAGE, AND OPEN MY HEART AND MY HOME. BECAUSE OF THAT HOPE, I COULD EMBRACE YOU FULLY. BECAUSE OF THAT HOPE, I COULD MEET WITH YOU AGAIN AND ENCOURAGE YOU AGAIN. BECAUSE OF THAT HOPE, I CAN SEE A DIFFERENT

END. BECAUSE OF THAT HOPE, I SEE YOU DIFFERENTLY FROM THE WAY YOU SEE YOURSELF. BECAUSE OF THAT HOPE, I KNEW YOU WOULD BE OK. BECAUSE OF THAT HOPE, I KNEW I WOULDN'T HAVE TO KEEP SAVING YOU FROM DROWNING, I JUST HAD TO TEACH YOU HOW TO SWIM.

BECAUSE OF THAT HOPE, WHEN IT GOT TOUGH, I REMAINED BUOYANT — BECAUSE HOPE FLOATS. THERE WILL COME A TIME WHERE YOU NEED MORE THAN THAT TINY GLIMMER, BUT FOR NOW, THIS IS WHERE WE START. IN YOUR OWN BEAUTIFUL WORDS: HOPE IS REAL, CHANGE IS POSSIBLE.

MUCH LOVE,

ESTHER

Esther doesn't just speak for our situation, to younger Jazz, but for you, too. As long as you are still here and you are still breathing, there is hope for you. Even in the darkest storm and when it feels like the world is better without you in it, there are people who care about and love you.

I have gone through a huge process to be living the life that I am now. But let me tell you this — you don't have to wait for life to turn around before you start making changes. You can sit there and think about wanting to change or dream about it, but <u>change doesn't happen until we actually physically do things to make it happen</u>.

An example for me is that I knew that I had a passion for TV and film. I decided to enrol in film school, and after I got

accepted, I began working my butt off. I would be the first
one to turn up and the last one to leave!

Not long after I started studying, my friend Genevieve and
I launched Voices of Hope, our mental health charity. When we
started, it was tiny — it was simply us trying to show people
that there was hope, and using our passion for storytelling to
do that. The first video that we made was one I directed,
called 'Dear Suicidal Me'. We had a budget of about $300,
brought a whole lot of students from my film school on board
and made a super-average-quality video.

That video ended up getting 80 million views across
different platforms. That year I became the youngest TV
director to win a national pitching forum, and as a result had
my show idea picked up. We began making more content for
Voices of Hope and were starting to slowly but surely make
some noise.

However, while all of this was happening, I was _still_ broke. I
was missing rent payments and was taking food home from
video shoots because I often couldn't afford to eat. In fact,
it actually wasn't until about 18 months ago that I started
making money and was able to get myself into a stable living
situation and even bought my first proper car!

I tell you this part of the story because I grew up very poor.
Poverty was simply a part of my life and was all that I had
known. I never actually expected that to change; I assumed I
would always live pay-cheque to pay-cheque, finding inventive

new ways to 'make do'. But even those things that seem so ingrained in us, which might seem to 'run in the family' or are common in our area, can also change.

During this time I was also actively trying to restore relationships, untangle the negative core beliefs that had made me suicidal for so many years, and trying to remind myself that I deserved to be here. It was one heck of a process and one that I am still working through (I am currently in trauma therapy, to ensure that I am continuing to grow and address things in my own life). However, if you told that girl sitting in that psych ward that one day she would live the life I have now, she would have never believed you. But hope is real, and change is possible.

I am not the only one with a story like this. In fact, the world is filled with them — including some names of people a lot of us would know.

LeBron James, for example. Many of you, basketball fans or not, would have heard his name. However, many of you may not know his story. He was born to a 16-year-old mother and his dad was an ex-con and absent from his life. His solo mum struggled to raise him after his grandmother died, and eventually he went to live with his football coach — who introduced him to basketball, and the rest is history. Hope is real. Change is possible.

Oprah Winfrey was initially raised by her grandmother, before moving around a lot between her parents as a child.

She was sexually abused at a young age, and got pregnant at the age of 14. But eventually Oprah became the first black female news anchor in her area, and then became a hugely successful daytime TV host, and the world-famous personality that we know today. Hope is real. Change is possible.

It may feel really dark for you right now, but there is always hope for change. Change doesn't necessarily mean 'success' — but it does mean that in time your life can look very different. The darkness can lift, relationships can be restored or put to rest. You can learn to smile again, laugh again and one day look back and say, 'Wow, I did that.'

While you are still alive and breathing, there is still a chance for change. It doesn't have to be like this forever, and it won't be like this forever.

Don't give up. Anything is possible.

Hope is real. Change is possible.

All my love,

Jazz

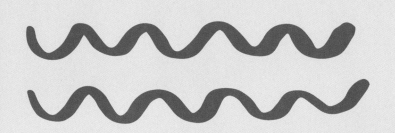

HOPE FLOATS.
IT'S BUOYANT,
ABLE TO STAY
ABOVE THE
WATER, EVEN
IN A STORM.

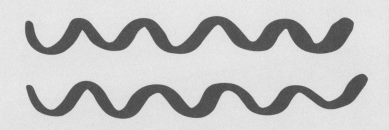

PART 4:

Help

To read if you are a parent

Hi there!

I wanted to put this letter in here specifically for parents to read — parents who have kids that are struggling and maybe feel overwhelmed themselves, or at a bit of a loss as to what they are supposed to do. I am not a parent myself, so I can only imagine how difficult it must be to watch your child struggle and feel like you don't know how to help. Almost every day I hear stories of parents who don't know what to do and are feeling all kinds of emotions and confusion about what is going on with their child.

I want to introduce you to Wayne and Libby. If you have heard of my story before you may have heard of them, but if not, let me tell you a little about them. I first met Wayne and Libby when I was 16 years old, through the church that we all went to. I was a very broken, very mentally unwell teenager who was caught in a cycle of hurting myself and trying to hide my true feelings and situation from everyone around me. After a few years, Wayne and Libby became like parent figures in my life and now, ten years later, are the people I consider family.

They have two children of their own, but they chose to open up their home and their hearts to not just me, but a few different young people. They have walked with me through the darkest parts of my journey, visiting me in the ICU of a psych ward and spending many, many nights with me, when I was crying at their house. We have navigated through so much, with me throwing up defences and masks, lying and trying to run away — but through it all, they never gave up on me.

They are not mental health professionals, but they do know what it is to love unconditionally, to both validate and challenge emotion and, very simply, have shown the power of consistency, compassion and 'showing up'.

That's why I have asked them to write you this letter — <u>from</u> parents <u>to</u> parents. I may not know what it is like to have kids (biological or 'adopted'), but they do. I hope that you find Wayne's words here (and Libby's, on page 175) comforting and encouraging.

DEAR MUM AND DAD,
IT'S REALLY IMPORTANT RIGHT NOW FOR YOU TO REMEMBER THAT YOUR CHILD DOESN'T KNOW YOU THE WAY YOU KNOW THEM.

YOU'VE KNOWN THEM SINCE DAY ONE. YOU'VE HAD ALL OF THEIR YEARS TO LEARN THEM — THEIR PERSONALITIES, QUIRKS, LIKES AND DISLIKES, STRENGTHS AND WEAKNESSES. YOU'VE SEEN THEIR LIMITS AND BOUNDARIES, THEIR FEARS AND JOYS.

THEY, HOWEVER, HAVE NOT LEARNT YOU THE WAY YOU HAVE LEARNT THEM. THEY MAY KNOW YOU LOVE THEM BUT THEY HAVE NO CONCEPT OF THE EXTENT OF THAT LOVE. THEY DON'T KNOW THE DEPTH OF LOVE AND COMMITMENT A PARENT HAS FOR THEIR CHILD. THEY ARE NOT AWARE OF THE LENGTHS YOU ARE PREPARED TO GO TO, TO SEE THAT THEY ARE SAFE AND CARED FOR AND WHOLE. THEY DON'T KNOW THIS ABOUT YOU ... YET.

THEY'RE STILL COPING WITH THEIR DEVELOPING BRAINS AND BODIES. HORMONES, PUBERTY, CHEMISTRY ... LET ALONE ANY EMOTIONAL TRAUMA THEY MAY HAVE BEEN THROUGH.

THEY DON'T EVEN KNOW WHAT THEY NEED OR WHAT IT IS THEY'RE REALLY CRAVING WHEN THEY DO HARMFUL THINGS TO THEMSELVES, SO OF COURSE THEY'RE NOT CAPABLE OF UNDERSTANDING THE DEPTH OF THE LOVE OF THEIR PARENTS YET. BUT THEY WILL, IF YOU TAKE THIS WINDOW OF OPPORTUNITY AND LOVE THEM CONSISTENTLY.

RIGHT NOW THAT'S ALL THEY NEED TO KNOW. AND THERE'S NO ONE MORE QUALIFIED THAN YOU TO LET THEM KNOW THIS.

THIS IS YOUR TIME TO SHOW THEM — TO TEACH THEM THAT WHEN EVERYTHING IS TELLING THEM TO RUN, THERE'S NO SAFER PLACE ON THE PLANET THAN YOU. THAT IN THE SAFETY OF YOUR EMBRACE AND PROTECTION THERE IS NO <u>JUDGEMENT</u>, JUST <u>UNCONDITIONAL LOVE</u>. THAT YOU'RE NOT ANGRY; INSTEAD, YOU'RE COMMITTED TO THEM TO THE END. THAT NO MATTER WHAT THEY DO, YOU'RE ALWAYS THERE AS A SAFE PLACE,

WHERE A SIMPLE HUG CAN DO MIRACLES FOR THE SOUL. WHERE A SIMPLE MEAL (WITHOUT AN ACCOMPANYING LECTURE) CAN FEED MORE THAN THE BODY. WHERE HOME MEANS REST, PEACE, SAFETY AND UNDERSTANDING; A PLACE TO REGROUP, TO 'FORTRESS' AWAY, TO MAKE A PLAN OF BOTH DEFENCE AND ATTACK WITH THEIR GREATEST ALLIES — YOU!

THEY WILL LEARN THAT CONSISTENT AND SACRIFICIAL LOVE DOES WHATEVER IT TAKES TO HELP THEM MAKE IT THROUGH. IT WILL NEVER LEAVE, NEVER FORSAKE. THEY WILL LEARN THAT YOU THINK THEY ARE <u>WORTH</u> SACRIFICING TIME, AFFECTION, MONEY AND EMOTIONAL ENERGY ON.

I'VE GOTTA SAY, I THINK I'M A PRETTY GOOD DAD BUT I CERTAINLY DON'T HAVE ALL THE ANSWERS. IN FACT, THE BIGGEST MISTAKES I'VE MADE WERE WHEN I TRIED TO BE SOMETHING I WASN'T: A COUNSELLOR, PSYCHOLOGIST, NUTRITIONIST, DOCTOR, MANAGER. I WAS BEST WHEN I WAS JUST DAD.

YOUR KIDS DON'T NEED YOU TO BE ALL THAT OTHER STUFF; THEY JUST NEED TO KNOW THEY ARE LOVED AND ACCEPTED, AND NOT REJECTED BY YOU. THEY NEED TO KNOW THAT WHEN THEY THINK THAT EVERYBODY IN THE WORLD IS REJECTING THEM, <u>YOU</u> ARE NOT. THAT WHEN THEIR HEAD IS FILLED WITH CHAOS, THAT YOU ARE A SAFE PLACE TO RUN TO AND TO HIDE IN.

YOU SEE, SOMEWHERE ALONG THE LINE, FOR WHATEVER REASON, YOUR CHILD STARTED BELIEVING SOMETHING THAT ISN'T TRUE. THAT THEY'RE WORTHLESS, ALONE, REJECTED, NOT ACCEPTABLE. EVEN THOUGH <u>YOU</u> KNOW IT'S NOT TRUE, THEY ACTUALLY BELIEVE IT IS. IT HAS BECOME A CORE BELIEF, PROBABLY TRIGGERED BY AN EVENT OR SERIES OF EVENTS, THAT HAS GROWN INTO A DESTRUCTIVE LIE, WREAKING HAVOC WITH THEIR EMOTIONS, SELF-WORTH AND IDENTITY.

ONE DAY IT'S GOING TO BE IMPORTANT TO GET TO THE ROOT CAUSE OF THIS BELIEF, AND I WANT YOU TO KNOW THAT WHEN THAT TIME COMES, THERE IS HELP AND SUPPORT, BOTH PROFESSIONAL AND VOLUNTARY, OUT THERE FOR YOU TO NAVIGATE THIS, BUT RIGHT NOW THAT'S NOT THE MOST IMPORTANT THING. RIGHT NOW YOU ARE THE MOST QUALIFIED PEOPLE TO VALIDATE THEIR EMOTIONS, BUILD THEIR SELF-WORTH AND AFFIRM THEIR IDENTITY AS A LOVED AND TREASURED SON OR DAUGHTER. RIGHT NOW YOUR RESPONSIBILITY IS TO LET THEM KNOW THAT THEY ARE SEEN, THEY ARE HEARD AND THEY ARE BELIEVED. THEY NEED TO KNOW THAT THEY ARE NOT ALONE — THEY ARE COVERED AND PROTECTED!

SOMETIMES THEY'LL REJECT YOU. THEY MAY YELL OR SCREAM OR RESIST. PLEASE SEE BEYOND IT. THEY DON'T KNOW WHAT THEY'RE DOING. IT'S JUST A DEFENCE SYSTEM THAT YOU'LL NEED TO SLOWLY MELT WITH CONSISTENCY OF THE SAME MESSAGE, OVER AND OVER AGAIN. A BABY BIRD WITH A WOUNDED WING DOESN'T NEED TO BE SCOLDED FOR FRANTICALLY FLAPPING ABOUT IN PANIC AND FEAR. YOU NEED TO SEE BEYOND THE FRANTIC AND KEEP REAFFIRMING: 'IT'S OK, YOU'RE SAFE, YOU DON'T HAVE TO DO THAT. I'M NOT GOING ANYWHERE, I'M HERE FOR YOU, I LOVE YOU AND NOTHING YOU COULD DO WILL CHANGE THAT.'

JUST ONE LAST THING. YOU MAY FEEL LIKE BLAMING YOURSELF FOR SOME OR ALL OF WHAT THEY'RE FEELING. MAYBE YOU HAVE HAD SOME DEGREE OF RESPONSIBILITY IN IT ALL, OR MAYBE YOU HAVE NONE AT ALL! REGARDLESS, ALL OF THAT IS SIMPLY NOT HELPFUL TO THEM RIGHT NOW SO, AS HARD AS IT IS, PLEASE TRY TO PUT THAT ASIDE FOR NOW. <u>IT'S NOT ABOUT YOU.</u>

MUM, DAD — YOU CAN DO THIS. ASK FOR AND SEEK HELP FOR YOU

BUT ULTIMATELY JUST <u>BE</u> FOR THEM. <u>BE</u> THEIR MUM AND DAD, AND COVER THEM. <u>BE</u> THEIR SAFE HAVEN, <u>BE</u> THEIR NURTURE AND PROTECTION, <u>BE</u> THEIR UNCONDITIONAL LOVE AND <u>BE</u> THEIR VOICE OF TRUTH IN AMONGST ALL THE OTHER VOICES.

GIVE THEM VISION WHEN THEY CAN'T SEE, AND A HAND TO HOLD WHEN THEY'RE STUMBLING IN THE DARK. THEY WILL KNOW HOPE WHEN THEY HEAR HOPE'S VOICE THROUGH YOU.

CHEERING YOU ON FROM HERE,

WAYNE

I think that one of the most important things that Wayne and Libby did for me was create a space that ensured that no matter what I had done or how I had screwed up, I knew that I could always go to them and be safe. This meant that I wasn't trying to hide things or trying to cope by myself. It meant that it was easier for me to keep open communication with them, and to reach out to them before things got worse. This was a process for me to learn, but over time I did begin to realise that I could go to them before things imploded. I knew that I would never be met with 'things could be worse' or 'it's not that bad' or anything like that — just open arms, validation and then 'where to next?'

If your child asks for help, give it to them. Take them to the doctor, let them see a counsellor, validate them. Don't let your fear of professionals thinking that somehow you have failed as a parent prevent your child from getting help. The professionals don't think that. There are so many reasons that your child could be struggling, and if they ask for help it is so important that you do your best to give it to them. Otherwise, the next time they may not come to you.

Lastly, remember that your feelings are valid too. As Wayne mentioned, it is OK for you to also seek help and support during this time. You are not alone in what you are feeling and you may actually find that seeking help, whether from a professional or trusted family and friends, may enable you to understand and respond better.

You can't help someone from an empty cup. You are important too and your frustrations, fear, exhaustion and confusion are all understandable — and you don't need to feel them alone.

Ask for help.

Love your child.

Never give up.

You've got this,

Jazz

YOU CAN'T
HELP SOMEONE
FROM AN
EMPTY CUP.

To read if you have a friend who is struggling

Hi there!

I am really glad that you turned to this letter — this shows that you really care about your friend and that you want to know how to help. You are a really good friend — thank you.

There are so many different things that you can do when a friend is struggling, depending on the situation and the severity of what they are struggling with. I want to be as practical as I can with you in this letter, as I know you came to this for tools and tips, so I want to tell you everything that helped me and things that I have learnt from helping others.

The first thing that you must know is that you as an individual cannot save your friend. That is not your job, nor is it possible. You are not a super hero, you are not a therapist, you are their friend, and they need you to be just that. Their <u>friend</u>. You are there to be an ear, to walk with them, love them and, when needed, point them in the direction of professional help.

There are many things that those around me did that really helped me when I was in the midst of my struggle. One of them in fact is partly what inspired this book. As you may have read earlier, a friend of mine, Cahlia, wrote me a whole lot of letters titled 'To open when you are feeling . . .' There were about eight of them, each one for me to open when I was feeling a certain way — 'To open when you are feeling unlovable', 'To open when you are feeling like you are not enough', etc. In each envelope was a letter that she wrote about that particular feeling, encouraging me and reminding me of little practical things that I could do in those moments. There was also a little quote card in each envelope and a photo of us together. This is something super-practical that you might want to do for your friend who is struggling. For me, it was something I held onto that enabled me to feel like I wasn't alone in my battle.

A more simple thing that one of my friends did was send me a text message every couple of days, just to check in and remind me that she loved me. At times I wouldn't respond, but when I got a message I knew that she was there and that she was thinking of me, which also helped start to shift my core belief that I was alone. This friend of mine knew that I had this negative core belief — the feeling that I was unlovable and a burden to people around me.

Often those who are suffering may be struggling with these similar beliefs, so constant, gentle contradictions to the beliefs can have more impact than you will ever know. This is important in what you say but also in how you act — not only telling them they are valued but also <u>showing</u> them, by including them in things, listening to them when they want to talk and helping them get support. You are not solely responsible for changing their core beliefs, but you do have the important role of being part of challenging those beliefs.

Don't be afraid to ask them what they need from you. Sometimes they might want to be distracted and go do something fun; other times they may want advice; or they might just need you to listen and be an ear for them to vent to. Sometimes we can get into the habit of thinking that people want us to fix everything when they come to us, but often they simply need to be heard.

If you are really worried about their wellbeing and think they might need professional help, then it is a good idea to suggest that to them. However, you need to do this in a way that is not patronising, but coming from a place of concern and love. Other practical things are sitting with them while they make the call, offering to drive them to their appointment, planning to hang out with them before or afterwards, or even sending them a message or calling to check in and see how they are doing. Doctors are always a good starting point for seeking help, as they are able to point your friend in the direction of what kind of help they need. Whether it be counselling, medication, life tips or more hands-on or serious help, they will be able to assess that.

Walking with someone who is struggling can be difficult, I know that. It can feel tiring and emotionally draining at times — so make sure that in all of this, you are also seeking support when <u>you</u> need it and taking care of your own wellbeing. This will help protect both you and your friend or loved one.

There are so many resources out there — stories of other people who have fought through struggles and made it to the other side; guides on how to help and how to be there for someone; information and help for those struggling. Do some research and know that you are not doing this alone.

You are not their saviour. You are their friend.

Walk with them, love them, listen to them and lend a helping hand where you can.

We are all in this together.

Much love,

Jazz

IT IS NOT YOUR JOB TO SAVE SOMEONE. IT IS YOUR JOB TO *love* THEM, *listen* TO THEM AND *support* THEM.

To read if you are scared to tell your parents how you are feeling

Hi there!

I am not going to write too much in this letter, as I wanted to have someone who is a parent talk to you — someone who knows what it's like having children and who might be able to encourage you to have the courage to speak up and talk to your parents. This letter is from Libby, who became like a mother to me when I was struggling. What she has to say is really important — so make sure you read carefully!

   Much love

   Jazz

HEY SWEETHEART,

I'M A MUM, AND A PRETTY SENSITIVE ONE AT THAT. I FEEL OTHERS' EMOTIONS, I CAN SENSE THE ATMOSPHERE OF PLACES I WALK INTO, AND I

HAVE A HEART TO HELP PEOPLE NAVIGATE HARD THINGS.

AND I LOVE MY KIDS! THIS JOURNEY OF LOVE AND CARE IS A LIFELONG PRIVILEGE AS A PARENT.

YOU ARE WORTHY OF THAT LOVE, _YOU_ ARE WORTHY OF THAT CARE, AND _YOU_ DESERVE TO FEEL SAFE, SEEN AND HEARD.

FROM A YOUNG AGE, WHEN ONE OF _MY_ KIDS WAS STRUGGLING, MY INSTINCT WAS TO WANT TO FIX THEIR PROBLEM, FIND A SOLUTION, TAKE THE PAIN IF I COULD, AND NEVER HAVE THEM EXPERIENCE THE HARD THINGS THAT WERE CAUSING THAT PAIN. MY BIGGEST DESIRE WAS THAT THEY WOULD FEEL SAFE, SECURE AND HAPPY, AND THAT THEY WOULD KNOW THAT HOME, AND WE AS PARENTS, WAS THAT SAFE PLACE FOR THEM.

EVEN WHEN THEY WERE SMALL, WHEN I COULD SEE PAIN IN THEIR EYES OR HEAR IT IN THEIR CRIES, IN JUST THESE LITTLE THINGS, IT BROKE MY HEART. YOU NEED TO KNOW THAT SOMEONE'S HEART BREAKS OVER YOUR PAIN, TOO.

AS MY KIDS GOT OLDER, LIFE HAPPENED TO THEM. MY HEART HURT AS I SAW THEM WRESTLING WITH GROWING UP AND BEING CONFRONTED WITH SITUATIONS THEY SHOULD NOT HAVE TO DEAL WITH. I STILL WANTED TO FIX THEIR PROBLEMS, FIND A SOLUTION, AND TAKE THE PAIN SO THEY WOULDN'T HAVE TO EXPERIENCE THE HARD THINGS ANYMORE.

I WANTED THEM TO KNOW THAT THEY COULD TALK ABOUT ANYTHING WITH ME — THAT NO SUBJECT WAS TOO HARD, OR TOO SHOCKING, AND THAT I WOULD ALWAYS LISTEN. I WANTED THEM TO KNOW THEY WERE NEVER A BURDEN. I HAD TO WRESTLE WITH MY OWN SITUATIONS AND PAIN GROWING UP, AND I WANTED TO BE ABLE TO TELL THEM THAT IT WAS GOING TO BE OK — THAT IT WAS POSSIBLE TO SEE BEYOND THIS SEASON OF PAIN

AND KEEP HOPE IN THEIR HEARTS. I WANTED TO BE ABLE TO ASSURE THEM
OF THAT, BECAUSE OF WHAT I HAD EXPERIENCED. HOPE IS REAL, AND HOPE
IS POWERFUL, AND IF YOU CAN HOLD ON, WITH GOOD PEOPLE AROUND YOU,
THIS SEASON WILL PASS.

BUT EVEN THOUGH I LET THEM KNOW THEY COULD TALK TO US
ABOUT ANYTHING, THERE WERE TIMES WHEN THEY DIDN'T, AND THAT WAS
THE HARDEST THING FOR ME. MAYBE THEY FELT THEY COULDN'T TALK
BECAUSE THEY DIDN'T HAVE THE WORDS, OR MAYBE THEY FELT I WOULDN'T
UNDERSTAND WHAT THEY WERE FEELING AND EXPERIENCING, OR MAYBE
THEY THOUGHT I WOULD BE ANGRY AT SOMETHING THEY HAD DONE AND
THAT WOULD AFFECT MY LOVE FOR THEM.

THOSE MIGHT HAVE BEEN REAL EMOTIONS AND FEARS, AND NATURAL
RESPONSES, BUT THEY WEREN'T TRUE. AND I COULD TELL WHAT THEY
WERE FEELING ANYWAY — BELIEVE ME, YOU DON'T NEED ONLY WORDS TO
COMMUNICATE YOUR FEELINGS. I COULD FEEL WHEN THEY WERE DISTANT
AND SCARED, I COULD FEEL WHEN THEY WERE HIDING AWAY IN SHAME OR
FEAR, I COULD FEEL THEIR PAIN ... AND EVERY PART OF ME WANTED TO FIX
THEIR PROBLEM, FIND A SOLUTION AND TAKE THEIR PAIN.

MORE THAN ANYTHING, I WANTED TO WRAP THEM UP AND KEEP THEM
SAFE. BUT I KNEW I COULDN'T, BECAUSE LIFE HAPPENS.

SO, THE BEST THING I COULD DO AS A PARENT WAS TO REASSURE
THEM THAT I WAS ALWAYS THERE FOR THEM NO MATTER WHAT, AND THAT
I WANTED TO WALK THEIR JOURNEY ALONGSIDE THEM. THAT THEY WERE
LOVED, ACCEPTED AND SAFE WITH US. NO MATTER WHAT ...

FEAR, SHAME, SECRETS AND PAIN WILL DO ALL THEY CAN TO KEEP YOU
LOCKED UP INSIDE YOURSELF. AND THAT'S A HORRIBLE PRISON TO BE IN.

AS A MUM TO A CHILD, I WANT TO ENCOURAGE YOU — PLEASE TALK, PLEASE REACH OUT, PLEASE LET SOMEONE INTO THAT PRISON YOU HAVE LOCKED YOURSELF IN. YOU ARE <u>NEVER</u> A BURDEN, AND YOU ARE <u>NEVER</u> TOO MUCH. THERE ARE PEOPLE WHO LOVE YOU EXACTLY AS YOU ARE RIGHT NOW, EVEN IN THE MIDDLE OF YOUR JOURNEY, AND WANT TO WALK WITH YOU THROUGH IT, TO THE OTHER SIDE.

I UNDERSTAND THAT YOU MAY NOT HAVE A BIOLOGICAL PARENT WITH WHOM YOU FEEL SAFE — THEY MAY HAVE BEEN PART OF YOUR JOURNEY OF PAIN IN SOME WAY. BUT I KNOW THERE WILL BE SOMEONE YOU CAN TURN TO AND REACH OUT TO. PLEASE LOOK FOR THOSE PEOPLE, AND TRUST THAT THEY CAN SEE THROUGH YOUR MASKS, DEFENCES, BEHAVIOUR AND FEAR, AND THEY WANT TO LOVE YOU AND WALK WITH YOU REGARDLESS, BECAUSE YOU ARE WORTH IT.

YOU ARE LOVED.

YOU ARE HEARD.

YOU ARE SEEN.

LET SOMEONE IN ...

YOU'VE GOT THIS!

LIBBY

YOU ARE
NOT
A BURDEN.

To read if you are scared to see a professional

Dear you,

I know that reaching out to a professional is scary. For some of you it's your first time, and for others, maybe you have tried to in the past but haven't had a great experience. I personally really struggled with and feared the idea of seeing a mental health professional for a long time. I had many preconceived ideas about them, thinking that they were only 'paid to care', but eventually, once I committed to going to see someone, I learnt how incredibly beneficial and helpful it can be once you find the right person.

To you who are considering reaching out but are afraid, here is what it looks like from the other side — a letter written by a therapist to a future client. I really hope it encourages you to reach out and get the help you need.

All my love

Jazz

HELLO THERE,

WALKING THROUGH THE DOOR FOR THE FIRST TIME INTO YOUR THERAPIST'S OFFICE CAN BE SCARY, AS YOU DON'T KNOW WHAT TO EXPECT. YOU MAY ALSO FEEL SOME HOPE THAT YOU MAY FINALLY BE ABOUT TO GET THE HELP YOU HAVE BEEN SEARCHING FOR.

I AM SITTING AT MY DESK, PREPARING FOR THE SESSION AHEAD, READY TO MEET YOU. I HAVE IN MY MIND THE IMPORTANCE OF THIS FIRST SESSION AND HOW I WANT TO CREATE A SPACE WHERE A RELATIONSHIP CAN DEVELOP THAT IS WARM, COLLABORATIVE AND OF COURSE EFFECTIVE IN GETTING YOU CLOSER TO YOUR GOALS AND A LIFE WORTH LIVING. I HAVE TO BE MINDFUL THAT I DON'T LAUNCH AHEAD WITH WHAT I THINK IS HELPFUL, BUT INSTEAD WALK THE JOURNEY ALONGSIDE YOU AND GUIDE YOU WHEN NEEDED.

I WANT TO HEAR WHAT YOU WANT TO GET OUT OF COMING TO THERAPY. I REALISE THAT THIS IS OFTEN NOT EASY TO SAY OUT LOUD, SO JUST TAKE YOUR TIME. I AM NOT AFRAID OF WHAT YOU HAVE TO TELL ME. THIS IS A SAFE SPACE TO TELL YOUR STORY... AND FEEL EMPOWERED TO SHARE EMOTIONS, THOUGHTS AND EXPERIENCES. WE ARE GOING TO FIGURE OUT TOGETHER WHAT LED YOU TO THE PLACE YOU ARE IN RIGHT NOW AND HOW THAT MAKES SENSE, ALL THINGS CONSIDERED.

YOU MAY BRING WITH YOU SO MANY PRECONCEIVED IDEAS OF WHAT LIES AHEAD. INFLUENCES LIKE YOUR PAST THERAPY EXPERIENCES (SUCCESS OR FAILURE) COME WITH YOU INTO THE ROOM. YOU MAY FEAR BEING MISUNDERSTOOD. THAT FIRST IMPRESSION YOU HAVE IS IMPORTANT, AND THIS CAN BE INFLUENCED BY WHAT YOUR THERAPIST SAYS, THE SPACE THEY GIVE YOU TO TALK, AND HOW THEY SUMMARISE YOUR EXPERIENCE. SOME MAY HIT THE MARK AND OTHERS MAY BE OFF. IF THEY ARE, IT IS

IMPORTANT TO SPEAK UP AND LET THEM KNOW THEY HAVEN'T GOT IT QUITE RIGHT.

REMEMBER YOU ARE NOT ALONE. STEPPING INTO THIS SPACE WHERE YOU ARE VULNERABLE AND SHARING WHAT IS MOST PERSONAL TO YOU IS COURAGEOUS AND STRONG.

TRUST IS A WORD THAT IS OFTEN USED. REMEMBER IT DOES NOT HAVE TO HAPPEN STRAIGHT AWAY. ALLOW A SPACE TO BE CREATED WHERE TRUST CAN GROW. ASK QUESTIONS LIKE 'WHAT WILL THE SESSIONS BE LIKE?' AND 'WHAT ARE THE BENEFITS OF THERAPY?'. SOME EXAMPLES ARE: LEARNING NEW SKILLS TO MANAGE EMOTIONS AND THOUGHTS, FEELING VALIDATED AND EMPOWERED, AND UNDERSTANDING THE DIFFICULTIES YOU ARE HAVING AND HOW THEY MAKE SENSE IN TERMS OF CURRENT OR PAST EXPERIENCES. LET YOUR THERAPIST KNOW WHAT IS HELPFUL OR NOT IN YOUR SESSIONS.

WHILE WE ARE PADDLING IN THIS WAKA TOGETHER, I WANT TO REMIND YOU THAT I DON'T WANT TO BE PADDLING IN A DIRECTION YOU DON'T WANT TO GO, WHILE YOU ARE BUSY DRILLING HOLES IN THE BACK AND I DON'T KNOW ABOUT IT! I WANT YOU TO TELL ME IF I AM PADDLING TO THE WRONG DESTINATION. I ALSO WANT YOU TO TELL ME IF YOU ARE FEELING THE URGE TO JUMP OUT. YOUR EXPERTISE ON WHO YOU ARE AND WHAT WORKS BEST FOR YOU WILL GUIDE US THROUGH.

TRY TO TAKE AWAY ONE THING TO REMEMBER FROM EACH SESSION. WRITE IT DOWN, AS IT IS EASY TO FORGET, AND DON'T FORGET TO PRACTISE WHAT YOU LEARN. THE GOAL OF THERAPY IS NOT TO GET RID OF ALL YOUR EMOTIONS... RATHER IT IS TO GENTLY MAKE ROOM FOR THEM.

I LOOK FORWARD TO MEETING YOU SOON.

DR KIRSTEN DAVIS

SHARING
WHAT IS MOST
PERSONAL TO YOU
IS COURAGEOUS
AND STRONG.

To read if you are afraid to see your doctor for help

Hi, friend!

Ah, yes — the fear of seeing your doctor when you are struggling with mental illness. This is something that I significantly relate to and struggled with for a lot of my life. I don't know what it was about medical professionals that scared me so much, but I often felt like a deer in the headlights trying to go in and admit to them that I was struggling. I personally had some past bad experiences with doctors, where I felt misunderstood and judged and almost 'tossed to the side', but what I came to learn is that most doctors do actually care about your mental wellbeing. They really do want to help you, but in order for them to help you, they need you to be honest with them.

By the fact that you are reading this letter I am assuming that you have been thinking about taking this step and seeing your doctor. This is a really important and vital step in getting professional help, as it is your doctor who will be able to help identify not only what might be wrong, but also refer you to places where you can access services like counselling. They can also help with medication if that is something you wanted to try, or can refer you to a psychiatrist if you need a more specialist doctor. The most important thing to remember is that they are there to help <u>you</u>.

I remember one time in particular that I was really struggling with my mental health, so much so that I got to the point of making a plan to take my own life. However, I found myself in my doctor's office, resentfully staring at the ground, refusing to make eye contact or even speak. I expected my doctor to just give me more medication and let me go on my way — but she didn't. She sat there talking with me, telling me of the future that I could have, and that I could make it through this but that I just needed help.

Hearing her talk like this was really confusing, as I had a mindset that doctors didn't actually care and just saw me as an inconvenience. However, this doctor, Doctor Steph, sat with me for what ended up being 90 minutes, telling me over and over again that I mattered and that I could get through this. Together we agreed on what was going to happen next, and she made sure I got the help I needed at that time. What I realised is that Doctor Steph, while not a mental health professional, was trained on what to do as the very next step.

A couple of years after this visit, I went back in to see Doctor Steph, this time for struggles around anxiety, feeling low and having trouble sleeping. From then on, the appointments I had with her would result in a medication change, a referral for further help or just some practical things that I could do to help myself. I began to learn the importance of going in to ask for help when I first felt I needed it, rather than waiting until things got too bad.

I will write more about this shortly, but first I asked Doctor Steph to write a letter for you from a GP's perspective. It shows you what they are often actually thinking and feeling, in the hope that after reading it you may feel a little more at ease to make the call and book an appointment.

DEAR PERSON WHO IS SCARED TO ASK FOR HELP,

FIRST, WHAT AN HONOUR IT IS FOR ME TO BE ASKED TO CONTRIBUTE TO THIS BOOK. SADLY, WHEN I FIRST MET JAZZ SHE WAS AT HER LOWEST. HER BODY LANGUAGE AND SPEECH MADE IT CLEAR TO ME THAT SHE DESPERATELY NEEDED HELP TO KEEP HERSELF SAFE.

AS WITH ALL MY PATIENTS, I TRIED TO REMIND JAZZ OF HER WORTH, AND THAT TIME COULD AND WOULD CHANGE HER VIEW ON LIFE, AND OF THE HUGE POTENTIAL THAT SHE AND EVERY ONE OF YOU POSSESSES, BUT WE NEEDED TO SUPPORT HER DURING THIS TIME.

WHAT I WANT YOU TO KNOW, AS A DOCTOR, IS THAT WE DO CARE AND WE ARE HERE TO HELP. MENTAL ILLNESS IS A HORRIBLE THING TO LIVE WITH BUT IS EQUALLY DIFFICULT TO TREAT WHEN WE DON'T KNOW EVERYTHING

THAT IS GOING ON. WE KNOW THAT YOUR ILLNESS CAN PLAY TRICKS ON YOU, SO OFTEN YOU MIGHT LACK TRUST IN OTHERS. IT CAN BE VERY HARD TO EXPLAIN TO SOMEONE WHO IS FEELING LOW THAT WE TRULY DO WANT TO HELP. NOT ONLY ARE WE TRAINED TO HELP, BUT THE REASON WE CHOSE THIS PROFESSION IS WE REALLY DO WANT TO HELP EVERYONE TO BE WELL AND LIVE A GOOD LIFE.

DON'T FORGET WE ARE HUMAN, TOO. I GO HOME FROM WORK AND OFTEN GO OVER SOME OF THE CONSULTATIONS FROM MY DAY IN MY HEAD, TRYING TO ANALYSE WHETHER I COULD HAVE SAID SOMETHING DIFFERENT, OR DONE SOMETHING DIFFERENT THAT MIGHT HAVE RESULTED IN A BETTER OUTCOME. PLEASE KNOW THAT WE WANT TO HELP YOU, BUT WE CAN ONLY KNOW AS MUCH AS YOU ARE WILLING TO SHARE. WE ARE NOT MIND-READERS! SO PLEASE BE OPEN WITH US AND LET US KNOW HOW WE CAN HELP, SO WE CAN TRAVEL THIS OFTEN-BUMPY JOURNEY TOGETHER.

YOU ARE NOT ALONE. WE ARE HERE TO HELP YOU.

DOCTOR STEPH

♡

We can only know as much as you are willing to share — this is a key thing to remember. Your honesty is so important when it comes to you being able to access the right help. You don't have to play down what you are feeling and experiencing — you are deserving of support.

A lot of people don't know that for the first few years that I was working as a mental health advocate I was still struggling at times with my own mental health, just not in such an extreme way. It would have been easy for me during that time to think 'It's not that bad' or 'I'm not in a high-risk situation, it's fine, I don't need help', but I learnt the hard way that it is far better to be proactive and to seek out help as soon as you notice that something is off — just like you would with your physical health.

For example, if you got an ear infection, you would go to the doctor and they would probably give you medication and tell you to rest for the course of the infection. With that medical help, eventually the infection would lessen and you would be OK. However, if you had an ear infection and you didn't go to the doctor because 'My ear hasn't been cut off' or 'Others need the doctor's time more than I do', then eventually that infection would get worse and you would end up far worse off, needing more extensive help than if you had gone when you first got the infection.

Sometimes we just need a bit of extra support to get us through a moment, whether that be counselling or medication — something to help you in the immediate future, then going on to work on some more long-term, long-lasting steps like counselling sessions and learning tools to help you to manage.

When I was in the middle of filming 'The Girl on the Bridge' I found myself starting to struggle with anxiety and had trouble sleeping. I ignored it at first, and then after a few weeks I got to the point where I was completely overwhelmed and stressed and felt like I was going to break down. I made an appointment with my doctor and laid down everything I was dealing with, and she was able to get me on interim medication to help and then direct me back into counselling.

I have now learnt the importance of asking for medical help when it's needed. These people are there to help you, but you have to <u>let them help</u>.

So whether you are in the middle of a storm and you are scared to tell your doctor, or if you are seeing your mental health starting to affect your life, then be brave and book that appointment. Go in, tell them the truth and let them help you. If you need to, take a support person with you.

You've got this.

Much love,

Jazz

SOMETiMES
WE JUST
NEED A BiT
OF EXTRA
SUPPORT
TO GET US
THROUGH
A MOMENT.

To read if you feel like your struggles aren't as bad as other people's

Hey!

First let me tell you: <u>your</u> trauma, <u>your</u> experiences, <u>your</u> emotions are valid. No matter what they are, you are so worthy of help. As someone who lived a lot of my teenage years suffering severe mental illness, and then also learning to navigate asking for help when I was no longer in crisis, I understand how easy it can be to just think 'Other people need the help more than I do'. However, I can tell you with full confidence that you are deserving of help — <u>no matter what it is that you are facing</u>. You don't have to do it by yourself.

The amount of times that I have heard people say 'My situation isn't that bad' or 'Others deserve the help more' is ridiculous. While absolutely there are people who have high needs, that <u>never</u> means that yours should be pushed to the side.

This same thinking is instilled into all of us as we grow up, when people tell you 'Others have it worse than you'. While this statement is true and it's good to remember that others are facing different battles, this comparison has created an entire generation of people who don't ask for help because 'others have it worse' or 'others need help more than I do' or 'I can just do it by myself'.

<u>Trauma is trauma</u>. What affects you deeply in life isn't going to be the same as what affects me. But someone who is struggling with anxiety for the first time is just as deserving of help and support as someone who has tried to end their life. Obviously different levels of support are required, but <u>everyone</u> is deserving of help.

When I was really battling, I struggled to ask for help. The mindset of 'others have it worse' or 'other people are the priority' meant that I often tried to manage on my own. And usually when that happened, my situation would go on getting worse because I wasn't getting the help I needed, and then it would turn into something bigger that I could have prevented had I spoken to someone earlier. However, I have come to learn the importance of speaking up and asking for help as I notice things starting to happen, rather than try to deal with it by myself.

Your feelings are valid. <u>You</u> are valid. It is OK to ask for help. Reach out. You've got this.

All my love,

Jazz

YOUR TRAUMA,
YOUR EXPERIENCES,
YOUR EMOTIONS
<u>ARE</u> VALID.

HOPE
ALWAYS
WINS

One final letter

Dear you,

Well, here comes the end of this book. It is my hope that the letters in it have been of help to you, and that it will continue to be of use going forward. This book was designed to be something that you read not just once, or in order, letter by letter, but something that is used again and again as a tool when you encounter different emotions and experiences, to help you feel just a little bit less alone.

Life has its ups and downs, and sometimes the downs can be really difficult to deal with. I'm a mental health activist who is known for surviving a pretty rough battle with mental illness, and even I still have bad days and have to do everything I can to pull myself back up. We are all humans trying to navigate life and all of the things that come with that. Don't be too hard on yourself — you are doing your best and I am really proud of you.

I hope that in your journey of reading this book that you have learnt some tools, felt comforted and understood that, no matter what you are facing or feeling, there is hope. You are so incredibly worth fighting for. Your life is so precious, and despite every hard thing that has come your way and all of the things you have had to go through in your life, you are still here, you are still breathing and that in itself is something so worth celebrating.

If there is anything I want you to know and feel as you read this last letter, it is that you are not alone. I may sound a bit like a broken record saying that over and over again, but that is because it is true. It is because I know first hand how lonely it can feel battling mental illness or difficult circumstances, and how that sense of being alone can make everything seem so much harder.

I remember being a teenager sitting in the psych ward and trying to research and find stories of people who had been through what I was going through. I spent so long wanting to find someone who I could relate to, something to make me feel less alone, but I couldn't find anything. Even just a few years ago, people didn't talk about mental illness because of the stigma attached to it, but now there are people from every corner of the world using their voices to share their stories — people from all stages of life and from all backgrounds who are choosing to speak up so that others may know that there is hope.

Feeling like you are the only one going through a tough time, or thinking that no one else behaves/responds/feels like you do can be so overwhelming and isolating, but you truly are not alone. There is an entire community of people who are fighting alongside you — <u>I</u> am fighting alongside you. Yes, there is hate in this world and there are situations and things that happen that are not fair, but what I have learnt and what I believe with my entire being is that hope always wins.

You are not alone.

Keep fighting, day by day.

You've got this.

All my love,

Jazz

Where to get help

1737, NEED TO TALK? — free call or text. Need to talk? 1737 is free to call or text from any landline or mobile phone, 24 hours a day 7 days a week.

ANXIETY NEW ZEALAND — 0800 ANXIETY (0800 269 4389).

DEPRESSION HELPLINE — 0800 111 757 or free text 4202 (to talk to a trained counsellor about how you are feeling or to ask any questions) (available 24/7).

HEALTHLINE — 0800 611 116.

KIDSLINE — 0800 54 37 54 (0800 KIDSLINE) for young people up to 18 years of age (available 24/7).

LIFELINE — 0800 543 354 (0800 LIFELINE) or free text 4357 (HELP) (available 24/7).

PARENT HELP — 0800 568 856 for parents/whānau seeking support, advice and practical strategies on all parenting concerns. Anonymous, non-judgemental and confidential.

RAINBOW YOUTH — (09) 376 4155 available 11 a.m. to 5 p.m., Monday to Friday.

RURAL SUPPORT TRUST — 0800 787 254.

SAMARITANS — 0800 726 666 (available 24/7).

SHINE (DOMESTIC VIOLENCE) — 0508 744 633 available 9 a.m. to 11 p.m., 7 days a week.

SKYLIGHT — 0800 299 100 for support through trauma, loss and grief; 9 a.m. to 5 p.m. weekdays.

SPARX.ORG.NZ — online e-therapy tool provided by the University of Auckland that helps young people learn skills to deal with feeling down, depressed or stressed.

SUICIDE CRISIS HELPLINE — 0508 828 865 (0508 TAUTOKO) is a free, nationwide service available 24 hours a day, 7 days a week, and is operated by highly trained and experienced telephone counsellors who have undergone advanced suicide prevention training.

SUPPORTING FAMILIES IN MENTAL ILLNESS — 0800 732 825.

THELOWDOWN.CO.NZ — or email team@thelowdown.co.nz or free text 5626.

WHAT'S UP — 0800 942 8787 (for 5–18-year-olds). Phone counselling is available Monday to Friday, 12 noon to 11 p.m. and weekends, 3 p.m. to 11 p.m. Online chat is available from 1 p.m. to 10 p.m. Monday to Friday, and 3 p.m. to 10 p.m. on weekends.

WOMEN'S REFUGE — 0800 733 843 (0800 REFUGE) for women living with violence, or in fear, in their relationship or family.

WWW.DEPRESSION.ORG.NZ — includes The Journal online help service.

YOUTHLINE — free call 0800 376 633, free text 234, talk@youthline.co.nz.

International

AUSTRALIA
LIFELINE — 13 11 14
KIDSLINE — 1800 55 1800
BEYOND BLUE — 1300 22 4636

USA
SUICIDE PREVENTION HELPLINE — 1 800 273 8255
CRISIS TEXT LINE — text HOME to 741741

UK
1 800 SUICIDE — 1 800 784 2433
1 800 273 TALK — 1 800 273 8255
UK SUICIDE HOTLINE — 08 457 90 90 90
CRISIS TEXT LINE — text 85258

CANADA
CRISIS SUPPORT — 1 833 456 4566
CRISIS TEXT LINE — text HOME to 686868

TOOLBOX OF HANDY SKILLS TO USE WHEN IN DISTRESS

BY CLINICAL PSYCHOLOGIST DR KIRSTEN DAVIS

A FEW NOTES ON THE HUMAN NERVOUS SYSTEM

First, I thought it would be helpful to explain a little bit about how our nervous system works, so you can see how the body and brain interact with each other. Our autonomic nervous system (ANS) runs our body behind the scenes. It is a control system regulating bodily functions, such as our heart rate, digestion and respiratory rate. It can be influenced by:

* the fuel we put in our body — food and water
* how active we are
* our emotions and thoughts
* our external environment.

It has both a sympathetic or stress-response system (SNS), which activates fight-or-flight responses and increases our emotional response; and a parasympathetic or relax-response system (PNS), which increases our emotional regulation and reduces emotional arousal.

When the SNS is engaged, our body goes into 'fight or flight' mode, stimulating the production of 'stress hormones' adrenaline and noradrenaline, accelerating our heart rate, relaxing our airways and dilating our pupils. When the PNS is engaged, we are able to 'rest and relax'. Our heart rate slows and we are able to digest food again.

The amygdala is part of the limbic system in your brain, and is involved in making memories and feeling pleasure, motivation and your emotions. It switches on when your SNS gets activated, as it thinks there might be danger. Sometimes it gets it right and other times not! When activated, it fuels your body with hormones, adrenaline and oxygen so you can be strong and fast and powerful. It revs up your brain.

Another part of your brain, the prefrontal cortex, slows it down, so you can be more mindful, think clearly and make better decisions to manage your emotions or urges. The practical tools included in this section are all ways to switch off the SNS and activate the PNS.

UNDERSTANDING YOUR 'SIGNATURE OF EMOTIONS'

When we experience an emotion, it creates a unique 'signature' in the body. Here are some ways in which different emotions may affect you physically. Use the following table to identify what emotion you are feeling in times of stress or crisis. What is your 'signature'? Highlight as you read.

EMOTION	TEMPERATURE/ FACIAL EXPRESSION / BREATHING / POSTURE / GESTURE/ MUSCLES / VOICE / ACTIONS
ANXIETY	* Increase in temperature (feeling hot/sweating, primed to run) * Red-faced, eyes wide, mouth slightly open * Rapid and/or shallow breathing * Tensed muscles * Biting your nails or your hands covering your mouth * Tense body posture — shoulders up, hands clasped, grip tight * Shaking, fidgeting, pacing, toes tapping, jumpy * High voice tone, or speechless * Being aware of the environment — watchfulness, checking, eyeing exit routes * Negative or distressing thought patterns — catastrophising, black-and-white thinking, 'what if's, uncertainty, thinking 'nothing is going to work out for me' or 'I won't be able to cope' * Avoiding — people, places, activities * Checking, seeking reassurance from others
SADNESS/GRIEF	* Downcast eyes, corners of the mouth turned down * Crying, or eyes misting over and tearing up * Loose, floppy body posture and muscles, sagging shoulders * Lying down or curling up in a ball * Moving slowly — feeling like you are dragging your body along rather than purposeful movement * Withdrawing * Low, slow voice * Seeking out reminders of the lost person — e.g. constantly looking on social media

SIGNATURE OF EMOTIONS

ANGER	
	✳ Clenched jaw
	✳ Narrowed eyes, frowning
	✳ Shallow breathing, 'huffing and puffing'
	✳ Rigid posture
	✳ Finger shaking, foot tapping
	✳ Tense muscles, fist clenched/raising
	✳ Physically confronting someone (being 'all up in their face') or turning away
	✳ Raised voice, snappy
	✳ Slamming doors
	✳ Shaking
GUILT	
	✳ Head down
	✳ Slower breathing
	✳ Hands open, arms spread and shrugging
	✳ Lower-volume voice
	✳ Tension in muscles
	✳ Apologising (perhaps over-apologising)

Source: Dunkley, Christine (2021), *Regulating Emotion the DBT Way: A therapist's guide to opposite action*, Routledge.

ADJUSTING YOUR EMOTIONS TO A LEVEL THAT FITS THE FACTS

The goal in managing anxiety, sadness, anger and other strong feelings is not to always get your emotional level down to zero. Instead, it is to *regulate* your emotion to a level that fits the facts of the situation.

When experiencing intense emotions, we need to figure out — does our emotion fit the facts or does the intensity of the emotion fit the facts? Then we can start trying to regulate our emotions to an appropriate level, through using the practical tools in the next section. You may need to ask yourself or someone else 'how much emotion makes sense in this situation?'. Sometimes it is hard to know, especially if you are in the middle of it all.

MAXIMUM EMOTION 100%

The amount of emotion is too high for the current situation.

To down-regulate the **excessive** amount of emotion, act opposite to the emotion's signature characteristics (see pages 203–204) until it fits the facts.

The amount of emotion roughly fits the facts for the current situation.

Utilise the valid amount of emotion to act on the situation and solve the problem if possible.

The amount of emotion is too low for the current situation.

If you feel the required amount of emotion is too low, reconsider the situation and make sure your reaction fits the facts. You may need to 'up-regulate' or increase the emotion.

MINIMUM EMOTION 0%

Source: Dunkley, Christine (2021), *Regulating Emotion the DBT Way: A therapist's guide to opposite action*, Routledge.

If your emotion fits the facts, then there are practical steps you can take to deal with the situation. If the emotion *does not* fit the facts, you need to change the way you are acting to change the way you feel.

Emotion: Anxiety

When does the emotion fit the facts?
When the health or life of yourself or someone you care about is in danger.

What to do when the emotion fits the facts:
If there is a real threat, be cautious, avoid or leave the situation.

Skills to use when the emotion doesn't fit the facts or you need to down-regulate it, as it is too intense:

* Reduce your body temperature — have a cold shower, drink a cold glass of water or use the Chill skill (see page 90).
* Slow down your breathing — use the paced breathing skill (see page 91).
* Change your body posture, e.g. relax your fingers, drop your shoulders, look up and focus on what is around you to take in important information that might show that the threat (e.g. people are laughing at you) is not reality.
* Relax areas of your body that are tense.
* If you are avoiding situations and/or people, first be mindful and aware that you are doing it. Notice the urge to avoid, run away or freeze. Now take the opposite action. What is the opposite action? To approach what you are avoiding, e.g. get out of bed

when you notice the urge to stay; set up a realistic daily schedule of what you are willing to do and check it off as you go.

* If you are frequently checking something — be aware once you have checked once, and avoid the urge to check again.
* If you are reassurance seeking — think about if this makes sense in the situation, as sometimes reassurance is helpful. If you are 'over-seeking' reassurance, then resist the urge to do it.
* Tolerate the anxiety by distracting yourself.

Emotion: Sadness or grief

When does the emotion fit the facts?

When there has been a loss.

What to do when the emotion fits the facts:

* Have a cry.
* Let yourself be sad — allow the sadness to come and go naturally. Notice when you are trying to push it down.
* Allow yourself some time out — lie down, read or watch a movie or series.
* Look at reminders of the person, and allow both happy and sad memories to come and go.

Skills to use when the emotion doesn't fit the facts or you need to down-regulate it, as it is too intense:

* Look up — be mindful and aware of your surroundings, to help get you out of your head.
* Half smile and relax your forehead.

* If you want to stop crying, use a cold face-mask or flannel, take deep breaths, focus on something else (distraction).
* Do the opposite action. If you feel the urge to wallow in your sadness, get out of bed. Plan to do something out of the house, like going for a walk. Use the paced breathing skill (see page 91). Plan a routine and stick to it. Say yes to going out. Exercise. Dance. Watch a funny YouTube clip.
* Be mindful (see page 217). Notice when you are starting to not want to do things and make an effective decision — what will work best for me right now?

Emotion: Anger

When does the emotion fit the facts?
When you are blocked from achieving a goal; when you or someone you care about is threatened; when you feel there has been an injustice or you are fighting for a cause.

What to do when the emotion fits the facts:
* Tolerate it — allow yourself to feel angry.
* Allow it — accept that you are angry.
* Self-validate (say to yourself 'It's OK to be angry at . . .').
* Stand up for yourself. Tell the person who has caused the harm how you are feeling, and ask for the situation to be repaired.
* Say no to things you don't want, or ask more firmly for what you do want.

Skills to use when the emotion doesn't fit the facts or you need to down-regulate it, as it is too intense:

* Talk normally, using a calmer tone.
* Notice the urge to bang or hit things, but instead walk away, letting your hands hang loose by your sides.
* Do the opposite action. Relax your face and body. Use the paced breathing skill (see page 91). Gently avoid situations that might make you angry.
* Be kind to yourself and others. Think about what good reasons could explain the other person's behaviour or what has happened. Imagine understanding why they behaved that way.

Emotion: Guilt

When does the emotion fit the facts?

When your behaviour has gone against your moral code or values, or against group norms (you have been caught gossiping about your friend, for example).

What to do when the emotion fits the facts:

* Repair the harm caused, if possible.
* Look for forgiveness.
* Accept the consequences that come your way willingly.
* Commit to not doing those behaviours again.

Skills to use when the emotion doesn't fit the facts or you need to down-regulate it, as it is too intense:

* Do the opposite action. Look up, and increase the volume of your voice. Search for what is true.
* Talk about what happened with people who you know won't reject you.
* Don't over-apologise for a harm you have not caused.
* If there is a chance that your behaviour might lead to rejection, you may make a decision to hide it, join a new group or try to change your group's values.

SOME PRACTICAL TOOLS

SENSORY STRATEGIES

Sensory input can be used to assist with self-regulation and supporting an 'alert-calm state'.

Calming sensory input is soothing, familiar, soft and rhythmic (for example, riding in a car, using a weighted blanket, chewing gum, slow rhythmic movements and dancing, massage, rocking, heavy and sustained resistance exercises).

Alerting sensory input is paced, quick, complex or unexpected (for example, jogging, looking at bright colours or fast dancing to your favourite song).

RELAXATION EXERCISES

Deep belly-breaths

Place a hand on your stomach, between your ribs and belly button. Place your other hand on your chest just below your collarbone.

Take a deep breath and notice what happens:

* Did you breathe through your nose?
* Did your shoulders stay still?
* Did your stomach expand first?
* Did you feel almost no upper chest movement?

If the answer to these questions is yes, then great — that's good belly-breathing. If the answer is no, practise some more!

Now, count your nice slow belly-breaths: each cycle of in and out counts for one. Count up to ten breath cycles. If you lose track of your count, go back and start at one again.

Another way to do it is nine-to-zero breathing, where again each cycle of an in-and-out breath counts for one, but count down from nine until you get to zero. Again, if you lose count, start back at nine again.

Visualisation exercises

Visualisation is also known as mental imagery and rehearsal. When you visualise you bring an image or series of images to your mind. Visualisation can include visualising the steps you will take to cope with a situation ahead of experiencing it, picturing a place where you have felt calm or other pleasant emotions (e.g. the beach, your bedroom), or guided visualisations where you 'walk through' completely new imagery (you can google a wide variety of these). Find one that works for you.

Calm mind / relaxed body

As you breathe in, say in your mind 'calm mind'. Breathe out and say 'relaxed body'. As you do this, drop your shoulders and relax your hands. Try doing this for five minutes.

COPING WITH PANIC ATTACKS

Right in this moment, do one thing at a time:

* Feel your feet on the floor.
* Observe your breath, and begin to take gradually slower breaths. Practise paced breathing (see page 91).
* Use the Chill skill (see page 90).

* Remind yourself that 'this too shall pass'.
* If you are hot, cool yourself down.
* If you are cold and shaky, warm yourself up.

MANAGING UNWANTED THOUGHTS

The experience of unwanted thoughts is common across all humanity. Do you ever feel pushed around by yours? Sometimes we become so 'hooked' and caught up in our thoughts that we don't even know we are having them. This can lead to us behaving in a way that takes us away from the sort of person we want to be and the sort of life we want to build. Sometimes our efforts to control these thoughts creates the very problem we are trying to resolve — they grow stronger and more relentless. Therefore, the goal is not always to make the thoughts go away, but rather to reduce the impact they have on you. Here are some different ways to change the way you relate to these unwanted thoughts:

* Invite them in with kindness and compassion. Hold the experience lightly and turn your mind to what will be meaningful to do in the next moment.
* Ask yourself: 'If you let that thought tell you what to do, will it take you in the direction you want to go to lead a meaningful life?' 'Does it help you deal with the situation if you hold on tightly to that thought?'
* Consider your values — what is important or meaningful to you? Are you heading towards living a life in line with your values?
* Check the facts of the situation. Are there alternative views or more information you need to take into account?

RADICAL ACCEPTANCE

Radical acceptance is the willingness to experience reality in our lives, ourselves and other people. It is accepting the things in our life that we can't change, big or small. It is not agreeing with, liking or being OK with what has happened or is happening, but accepting that we cannot change it. It is accepting from deep within: 'this is what it is'.

Fighting reality can turn pain into suffering. Pain cannot be avoided — it is nature's way of telling us that something is wrong.

Rejecting or fighting against reality does not change reality. Changing reality requires accepting reality. *The first step towards change is acceptance.*

Acceptance can lead to sadness, but a feeling of deep calm may follow.

Being mindful (see page 217) can help you find acceptance of the present moment — of reality as it is currently being experienced.

Practising acceptance

* Observe that you are questioning or fighting reality. Describe what happens when you are not accepting: thoughts, sensations, urges, actions.

* What would be different if you were accepting of your reality? What would you be saying to yourself: 'It is what it is'? Would your actions be different?

* Imagine in your mind's eye what you would be doing. Relax your face, drop your shoulders and pace your breath, breathing gently in and out.

* If you find yourself not accepting reality, then turn your mind back to acceptance.

FOCUSING ON THINGS YOU CAN CONTROL

In our daily lives there are many things that are within our control — that we can change if we want to. Consider the simple things that are part of your daily life: a good sleep routine, planning things you enjoy, listening to your favourite music, organising to spend time with family or friends. Turn your attention to these things and away from the things you can't control.

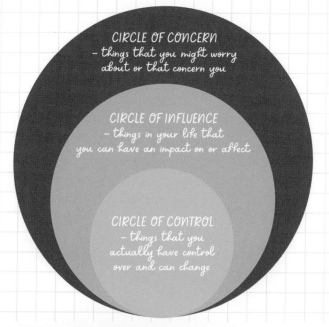

CIRCLE OF CONCERN
– things that you might worry
about or that concern you

CIRCLE OF INFLUENCE
– things in your life that
you can have an impact on or affect

CIRCLE OF CONTROL
– things that you
actually have control
over and can change

MINDFULNESS

Mindfulness is paying exquisite attention to this present moment. It is getting in control of your mind, rather than it being in control of you.

At its heart, it is a sense of oneness and connectedness with everything. The goal of mindfulness practice is mindfulness practice, and everything else that happens is a beneficial side effect. It is accepting that this moment is the only moment.

When you are being unmindful, it is easier to act on urges. Being mindful is noticing the urges and riding the wave of them, without acting impulsively.

Our minds often get stuck on thinking about what *might* happen or what *has* happened. Sometimes we then treat these thoughts as facts, when they are not.

Have you ever predicted that something bad was going to happen, and it didn't — like thinking people will laugh at you when you speak, and then you find out that they don't? Can you think of a time when your mind stopped you from saying or doing something?

Being mindful is noticing when your mind is caught in the past or future, or is distracted in this moment. Being mindful is noticing when you are on 'automatic pilot' and doing things you are not really aware you are doing, or losing time. It involves anchoring yourself in the present — being awake to and aware of this moment in time, and then acting skilfully. By being mindful you can work out what skills to use, and when, to keep your thinking under control.

Mindfulness is a skill you can learn, and the more you practise, the more you can weave it into your daily life. There are many mindfulness apps or examples of mindfulness exercises on the internet.

Mindfulness practice often starts with observing your breath. Use the one-to-ten or nine-to-zero techniques on pages 212–213 to help you focus and become calm.

To start with, maybe set a reminder on your phone. When it goes off, mindfully pause, and notice what you are experiencing, physically and mentally. Be aware of your thoughts, both the words and images. As you consider each one, say to yourself: 'I am noticing a thought that . . .', then let it pass like leaves on a stream. When you are being mindful, you can ask yourself 'Is this thought a judgement or a fact?', then consciously decide whether to act on these thoughts.

Mindfully focus your attention on the present moment.

In the here and now is where we are trying to be. You are being one-mindful, doing one thing at a time.

Notice when your mind drifts off and bring it back, again and again.

Don't judge. Observe judgements you might be making of yourself, others or your experience, stick to the facts, then let the judgements go.

Find which mindfulness exercises work for you. Keep in mind both your short- and long-term goals in choosing what to practice.

Understand your mind with curiosity. Pay attention to your thoughts. Watch them come and go like waves in the ocean.

Learn to accept that your mind will wander. Mindfulness will help you guide it back.

Notice what you can observe and describe using your senses.

Everyone has a 'wise mind' — a place of enlightenment where you clearly see the world and reality as it is. You might think of this as your 'heart of hearts', intuition or inner wisdom. Use this to guide your decision-making. Ask yourself 'what would my wise mind say right now?'.

Stay focused on your goals and stick with your practice.

Surprise yourself by focusing mindfully on pleasant experiences.

Acknowledgements

This book would not have been possible without quite a few incredible people who got in behind me and helped me create it:

First, to Dr Kirsten Davis and The Psychology Group for your professional input and adding practical tools for readers to use throughout this book. I have seen the amount of work, love, dedication and passion that you have for those battling mental health challenges, and the work that you do every day to help those struggling is incredible. Thank you.

To my wonderful supporters: you are the reason that I even had the opportunity to write this book in the first place. Thank you for giving me a platform to share my story, to talk about hope and to wake up every single day and do what I love most: help people. Many of you who follow me on social media had a big part to play in this book and helped make suggestions about what kind of letters you wanted to read. There were even those who sat on TikTok Live and ensured that I did not procrastinate while I was finishing this book! Thank you for being on this journey with me and allowing me to journey with you. I love you all and am so thankful for you.

Wayne and Libby Huirua — there are never words to express how thankful I am for you and everything you have done for me in my own world. Thank you for taking the time to write both to parents and on behalf of parents to try to help bring understanding, a fresh perspective and encouragement to families.

Genevieve Mora — thank you for using your story and past experiences to help those struggling with similar things with which you battled; for enabling people to hear from someone with lived experience and for them to know that there is light at the end of the tunnel. Thank you for choosing to fight for your own life and now choosing to fight for others.

Esther Greenwood — you know how thankful I am for you and how much you mean to me. You are a very, very significant part of why I am still here today, and many of the things you taught me through our journey have become the very pillars that I now stand on to create change. Thank you for opening the door even further in this book and allowing people to see our journey from your perspective, so that readers may know that despite feeling like they are a burden to people, they are not; for helping break down the perceptions, warped beliefs and fears that those struggling often have about those who are supporting them in their own journeys.

Doctor Steph — thank you for not only being the doctor who physically helped me many years ago, but for now choosing to be a part of creating change alongside me; for showing people that doctors can care, for taking it upon yourself to be a voice in changing the way doctors respond to mental health, and for being a kind, caring voice to those who are afraid to reach out.

Cahlia Southon — my wonderful friend who wrote me the first letters back in 2015. Thank you for sparking the entire idea for this book, for being such an incredible friend and for taking the time to write me the letters during the hardest time of my life. I am so thankful for you!

Thank you to every single person who was a part of this book and enabled me to create something that was not just for reading, but that held purpose and hope and ultimately is a tool to help people. Thank you for not shying away from talking about mental health, but fully embracing it, being willing to learn and never losing sight of the 'why'.

About Dr Kirsten Davis

Dr Kirsten Davis is a Clinical Psychologist with two decades of experience as a therapist, consultant and trainer in mental health and wellbeing across community and private settings. An expert in Dialectical Behaviour Therapy (DBT), specialising in working with adolescents, and Director/Trainer for DBTNZ and DBT Training Australia. Specific interests include the role of emotion regulation in suicide and self-harm behavior, and implementation of DBT.

Kirsten is also the co-founding Director and CEO of The Psychology Group (TPG), grown from her vision to bring together an expert team of highly qualified professionals, passionately dedicated to delivering accessible evidence-based therapies and training. TPG is committed to values prioritising collaboration, equal opportunity, diversity and cultural inclusivity. Kirsten cherishes friendship and family time, has two wonderful children, and loves time outdoors, running, gardening and reading in the sun.

About Jazz Thornton

Jazz Thornton survived a childhood of abuse, depression and chronic suicidal thinking to go on to have international influence in mental health and wellbeing, using her lived experience to help other young people. She has become a successful author ('Stop Surviving Start Fighting'), public speaker, award-winning web series director ('Jessica's Tree') and international mental-health advocate. A movie about Jazz and the making of 'Jessica's Tree' was released in 2020 — 'The Girl on the Bridge'.

Jazz is also the co-founder, along with Genevieve Mora, of the organisation Voices of Hope, which aims to remove the stigma around mental illness, and to show that hope is real and recovery is possible.

Jazz won Young New Zealander of the Year 2021 for her work.